REVIVAL FIRE NOW

Revival Fire Now: A Battle Call to Burn Until the Darkness Breaks

Copyright © 2024 Brian Bolt

All rights reserved. No part of this publication may be reproduced in a retrieval system, or transmitted in any form or by any means—electronic, mechanical, photocopying, recording, or otherwise—without the prior written permission of the publisher.

Scripture taken from the New King James Version®. Copyright © 1982 by Thomas Nelson. Used by permission. All rights reserved.

While precaution has been taken in the preparation of this book, the publisher and author assume no responsibility for errors or omissions, or for damages resulting from the use of the information contained herein.

This book is set in the typeface *Athelas* designed by Veronika Burian and Jose Scaglione.

Paperback ISBN: 978-1-967262-32-8

Produced in Partnership with *Tall Pine Books*
PO Box 42 | Warsaw, Indiana 46581

| 1 24 24 20 16 02 |

Published in the United States of America

REVIVAL FIRE NOW

A BATTLE CALL TO BURN UNTIL THE DARKNESS BREAKS

BRIAN BOLT

ENDORSEMENTS

I have traveled with Brian Bolt all over the world. I have been with him in the jungles of the Amazon, the dusty cities of Mexico, and the mountains of Western Uganda. I have done life with Brian Bolt. He's preached at my church and I have preached at his. I have hunted with him at Redemption Ranch. I say all this so that you know my endorsement is not just because I recognize his potential, I actually know Brian like a brother. Brian carries revival with him everywhere he goes. His life constantly convicts me to be a mighty carrier of the Holy Spirit and to bring the King's Kingdom everywhere I go. I can't wait for you to read this book.

Pastor Troy Brewer
Open Door Church
Burleson, Texas

Brian Bolt's book *Revival Fire Now* is like an ignition switch for us to become the witnesses that God has always intended us to be. All of us can raise the dead, all of us can cast out devils, and all of us can pray for the sick and see them healed. Brian is an amazing teacher and an amazing example of what it looks like to be a man on fire for the Kingdom. I would recommend this book to anybody that would like to grow in the fire of the Lord. This man is a blessing to the body of Christ. *Revival Fire Now* is a must read.

TODD WHITE

Founder and President of Lifestyle Christianity and personal friend of the amazing man of God who wrote this book

Revival has always been close to my heart. Whenever someone takes the time to write about revival, I want to read it—especially when I know the author and have seen firsthand what God has done through their life and ministry. *Revival Fire Now* by Brian Bolt is not just another book—it's a spark from someone who has carried the flame.

BISHOP TONY SUAREZ
Revivalmakers Ministries
Blountville, TN

From the very first line, you can feel the fire in these pages. This book is not theory–it's testimony, revelation, and impartation. Brian Bolt doesn't just talk about revival; he lives it. He writes from the battlefield of faith with the scars and the glory to prove it. *Revival Fire Now* is not for the casual believer. It's a clarion call to those who refuse to bow, quit, or cool down. If you're ready to burn with holy purpose and the power of Pentecost, this book will set you ablaze. Once this fire touches you, there's no turning back!

Dr. Medina Pullings
United Nations Church
Richmond, Virginia

After reading my friend Brian Bolt's book, *Revival Fire Now*, I am more ignited and determined to operate everyday in the realm of the miraculous for Jesus Christ. If you burn for the real power of God in your life, and you hunger for an encounter with supernatural demonstration, this is the book for you. I promise, you will not put it down. PHENOMENAL!

Bishop Jamie Tuttle
Dwelling Place Church
Cleveland, TN

As the world grows colder, God is raising up voices that burn. Brian Bolt is one of those voices. *Revival Fire Now* is a message born in the heat of battle and proven on the frontlines of faith. This is not a book for the average Christian. It's a trumpet blast to every believer who refuses to bow to apathy and longs to carry the fire of God into the darkest places. What I love about Brian's message is its refusal to settle for powerless religion. He reminds us that revival isn't an event to attend but a fire to embody. This fire is catching and as you read these pages, you'll feel that fire begin to stir in you.

Alan DiDio
Pastor of The Encounter Charlotte
Host of Encounter Today
Charlotte, NC

Revival Fire Now is a battle manual for those who refuse to bow. It ignites fresh fire, empowering believers with holy boldness and supernatural authority to dismantle darkness and advance God's Kingdom forward. Unashamed. Uncompromising. Unafraid.

CONTENTS

Foreword	1
Preface	5
1. The Call to Awaken the Fire Within	9
2. Holy Ghost Power That Shakes the Earth	21
3. Holy Ghost Fire That Devours Darkness	39
4. Heaven's Invasion Has Begun	63
5. History of Revival Fire	79
6. Prayer That Shakes Heaven and Dismantles Hell	103
7. Stand in Holy Boldness	127
8. Become a Torch of Revival Fire	161
Conclusion	189
Salvation's Call	197
About the Author	203
Notes	205

FOREWORD
BY DR. ROD PARSLEY

There are moments in the history of the Church that mark turning points, times when ordinary lives collide with supernatural purpose and the flame of Pentecost reignites in the earth.

I believe we are standing in such a moment now.

God has more for us than the hollow distractions and empty platitudes that fill our days, and more than the surface level faith that numbs our generation. There is a deeper call resounding again. It's a call to return to the upper room, to the raw, unfiltered presence of the Holy Ghost.

The Holy Spirit has not diminished with time. He has not grown silent or weary. He remains the same Spirit who raised Christ from the dead, who filled disciples with boldness, who turned fishermen into apostles and prayer meetings into outpourings. The Holy Spirit is not a relic of

Pentecostal memory. He is God, not a watered down version, but the all powerful, living God, the third Person of the Trinity, still speaking, still empowering, and still sending.

I have had the privilege of witnessing the fire of God consume lives, nations, and generations. For more than five decades, I have watched the Holy Spirit take what is broken and make it burn again. The faces change, the decades roll on, but the power remains unchanged. The fire never ages.

As Christians, we are children of The Cross, fruit of the empty tomb, and products of the upper room. The message of Pentecost affirms that the power of Pentecost is not confined to the pages of history but is a living reality for believers today.

The Church must once again embrace the mighty ministry of the Holy Spirit. It is He alone who is able to position us, prepare us, and empower us with supernatural direction to take complete advantage of every moment of kingdom advancement He affords us. He is working His plan even now for us to present the living hope of the gospel to a dying world with signs, wonders, and miracles following the proclamation of His word.

The final words encapsulated in Mark 16:15–16 remain our mission: "Go into all the world and preach the gospel to every creature. He who believes and is baptized will be saved, but he who does not believe will be condemned." Verse 20 continues, "Then they went out and preached everywhere, the Lord working with them and confirming the word through the accompanying signs. Amen."

This book carries Holy Ghost fire to encourage you in this mission. It calls believers out of spiritual survival and into Spirit filled dominion. It reminds us that the wind that rushed through Jerusalem will also rush through our cities, our churches, and our homes.

Are the events that transpired on the first Pentecost still possible today? Is that transformative power still available to the followers of King Jesus? If so, can we be used to change our world one life at a time here and now? It is my firm conviction that it is, that we can, and that we will, if only we are willing.

The world has lost its way, and the work of God is not finished.

In *Revival Fire Now*, Brian Bolt, a son in the faith, presents every believer with a provoking decision: burn with revival fire and change the world, or blend in and become a victim to its darkness. The Kingdom of God will advance. The only question is, will you be a part of it?

To those who read these words, expect to be challenged and changed. The Spirit of God is still writing the story of revival, one burning life at a time.

Dr. Rod Parsley
Pastor and Founder, World Harvest Church
Columbus, Ohio

PREFACE

This book was born in a fight. I wrote it with fire in my bones and a war cry in my spirit. I've seen too many believers quit when it got hard, back down when the pressure came, and silence the very fire God put in them. I can't do that. I won't. Quitting isn't an option for me because something inside me refuses to die. The fire of God keeps me alive, and that fire burns hotter when everything around me says stop.

Jesus said in Luke 12:49, *"I came to send fire on the earth, and how I wish it were already kindled!"* That's not soft, status quo, cookie-cutter, seeker-friendly language. It's a war cry. Jesus came to light the world on fire. And that fire is power. It's a refining flame that separates the real from the fake. When Jesus said He wished it were already kindled, He was looking ahead to The Cross because His death and resurrection would strike the match that would ignite the outpouring of the Holy Spirit. That fire burns in me and it's the reason I get up, the reason I preach, and the reason I don't quit.

The message of this book was branded into my soul after witnessing resurrection power firsthand. In June of 2025, during a crusade in Kenya, God told me weeks before I even stepped on the plane, "I will raise the dead in Kenya. That's how I'll mark this crusade." I didn't keep that word to myself. I declared it publicly. I told the church, "God will raise the dead in Kenya."

On the final night, the word became flesh. A young girl, sick for years, collapsed and stopped breathing. The medical team worked for nearly thirty minutes. Nothing. No pulse. No breath. No life. The air was thick with panic, but I knew what God had said. We had two choices: rush her to the hospital and lose her on the way, or bring her to the altar and believe God to do what He promised. She was carried to the altar. We laid our hands on her lifeless body, and we called on the name that conquers death. And in that moment, Heaven came down. The fire of God hit her, and breath came back into her lungs.

That little girl is alive and whole today. We still get videos. She's in school, running, jumping rope, and laughing. Whole. Healed. Alive. Jesus said, *"I have come that they may have life, and that they may have it more abundantly"* (John 10:10). This promise is true. It's a reality. I saw it with my own eyes.

That night, something changed in me forever. I can't ever go back to cold religion or powerless Christianity. I've seen the God who raises the dead. I'm provoked to action. I burn with an unquenchable fire that demands I keep moving. There is no revival without fire. There is no awakening without power. The fire of God is not an idea, it's the difference between life and death.

God is moving in power across the earth right now. He's looking for warriors, not for spectators. He's searching for men and women who will carry His fire with conviction and courage, who will not bow, who will not compromise, and who will set everything around them on fire with His presence.

As you read this book, expect to be shaken. Expect your excuses to die. Expect your heart to catch fire again. These pages carry a call to burn hotter, stand taller, and live bolder. My prayer is that you don't just read about revival, you become it. Once this fire ignites in you, you'll never be the same.

In these pages, you'll be stirred to hunger for God, to walk in power, and to see miracles flow through your hands. You'll be challenged to rise up in faith and not back down. You'll be empowered to advance God's Kingdom and change the world. The hour is upon us to stand up for God and righteousness. The greatest unused power in all the world lies dormant within the Church of Jesus Christ but Heaven and Earth are colliding once again and revival fire is igniting within the hearts of believers. And the Holy Ghost doesn't just ignite hungry hearts, He fills them, He transforms them, and then He sends them into the world with overflowing power.

Whether you're a pastor, a leader, or a new believer, *Revival Fire Now* will help you understand how God's fire, revival fire; empowers, how you can carry it wherever you go, and how you can burn for Jesus in a dark world.

We are in a sovereign outpouring of God. His Spirit is pouring out. Stop waiting for revival to come. Instead, surrender everything and become a torch of holy fire. There is more for you, in God, and you're about to step into it.

"Until my shadow heals the sick, there's more."–Brian Bolt

ONE
THE CALL TO AWAKEN THE FIRE WITHIN

"Revival comes from Heaven when heroic souls enter the conflict determined to win or die–or if need be, to win and die." –Charles G. Finney

There is a choice that confronts every believer. It's the choice between compromise or conviction. You have a choice. You can settle here or you can advance. You can go back to church as usual or you can take back everything the enemy has stolen from you.

Fire changes everything and within the heart of every born again, blood-bought believer of Jesus Christ, there is at least a spark of holy fire ready to be ignited. The voice of God is calling once again, not to the lukewarm or to the religious, but to those whose hearts still burn for Jesus. Heaven is searching for men and women who will refuse to be silent and who will not be satisfied until the fire of revival spreads like wildfire to the ends of the earth. It is a fact that when the Church loses her fire, she loses her power. But when one person decides to burn for God again, a spark can become a wildfire.

"For our God is a consuming fire."–Hebrews 12:29

The fire of God is transformational. It refines and consumes everything that is not of Him. In every era, revival began when God found a man or a woman willing to burn for Him. Before revival can fill a church, it ignites a heart. Revival begins in secret places of prayer where the soul cries out for more of God. It's born in repentance and in humility and it's maintained through radical and faithful obedience.

"Draw near to God and He will draw near to you."–James 4:8

The call for revival fire is not a call to a church service. It's a call to a surrendered, sold out life for Jesus Christ. It's not hype or emotion. It's becoming a holy sacrifice that allows God to take full possession of your life. Revival is the outcome of Heaven invading ordinary people and they are so fully transformed that they refuse to go back to normal and they change the world around them.

When a believer becomes consumed with Jesus, the fire within them becomes contagious and it spreads from heart to heart, home to home, and city to city until entire regions are marked by the presence of God.

For those who really want revival, it will cost you. The cheap, tearless, empty, burdenless, self-centered, watered down, crossless Christianity of our generation will never bring revival, reshape our generation, or change our world. You cannot build a strong house on a weak foundation. It will take more. So what will it take? What will it cost you?

I think it will take joining the ranks of the burdened; the uncommon men and women whose lives are lived so radically and devotedly that they are dangerous to the devil. They are committed. They are on fire. They love not their own lives even unto death. They will march to the very jaws of hell and pull people right out of the fire, no matter the cost.

That's what this generation is looking for. They are crying out like the Greeks cried out to Philip in John 12:21, *"Sir, we want to see Jesus."* They don't want your idle words and degrees. They don't want to hear about all the famous people you met. They don't want to hear your glory stories. No, they want to see Jesus.

This lost and wicked generation needs a revelation of Jesus–all loving and all powerful. The One who hates sin but loves the sinner. The One who finds us in our filth and sin and breaks every chain of the devil. The One who meets us in our darkest moments with the light of His love. The One who knows our every thought and loves us still. The One who endured mockery at the hands of the most vile so we could live free in this life and for eternity. The One who is patient when we run from Him but opens His arms wide and runs to us when we return. The One who was whipped and beaten so we could be saved, healed, and made whole. The One who even now anguishes in intercession for you; that you would know Him, live for Him, and then burn for Him.

This generation wants to see Jesus. They are looking for some people who will live as Jesus lived and pray as Jesus prayed. They are looking for some people who will love unconditionally. They are looking for some people who will forgive as Christ forgave and not be willing that any should perish but that all should come to repentance. They are looking for some people who will operate in power. They are looking for some people who will bring deliverance. They are looking for some people who will lead them to a baptism of fire. They are looking for some people who mean what they say and live it. They are looking for some people who have forsaken all else and pick up their cross daily. They are looking for some people who will not be shaken by the enemy or any trial they face. They are looking for some people who will not blend in with the world but will stand out and stand up for holiness and righteousness. They are looking for some people who are running into spiritual burning buildings and pulling others out of an eternal fire. They are looking for a Church alive with power and fire. That is what this generation is looking for–they want to see Jesus. And you can show them Jesus.

God is always seeking for and using yielded believers. God wants revival everywhere but needs empty vessels through whom He can flow. To burn with revival fire you lay yourself on the altar. You lose yourself in the God-given, Holy Spirit-inspired message of Jesus until the words become the living voice and power of the living Christ.

You lay yourself on the altar and you lift up Christ. *"And I, if I am lifted up from the earth, will draw all peoples to Myself (John 12:32)."* You hide behind The Cross and lift up Jesus higher and higher until He is made real to the people. But to do this, you must walk closely to Jesus; you must know Him, sharing in His love but also in His suffering and His grief over the state of the Church and the lost. This is the only way for you to be the instrument used for Jesus to become a living reality so near that this lost generation can reach out and experience Him, through you.

You lay yourself on the altar and, in exchange, receive anointing from above and utterance from within. When pouring out His revival Spirit, God's desire is to use us as His vessels, carriers, and instruments but only if we have committed to a personal pursuit of His Holy Ghost and fire. Even a sinner can tell in a moment if you have the oil and anointing of God. Rivers of living water have to flow. It is less important what flows from the head. What matters is what flows from your heart.

Revival fire causes you to become a messenger of salvation. The gospel must be shared. There must be a fearless, simple presentation of Bible truth: salvation by faith, healing for the body, the baptism of the Holy Spirit, and the coming of the Lord. Put away the scissors. Don't cut out what might offend. Don't remove the Holy Spirit and do not lower the standard of holiness. A clear dividing line must be drawn between the Church and the world, the sinner and the saint, and Jesus must be proclaimed as the only way a sin-burdened soul can find salvation and deliverance.

Revival fire will always produce a passion for souls coupled with the love of God. The foundation is the heart of the Father–soul winning and soul travail.

Revival fire requires you to put your all on the altar. In the Bible, altars are used for two things: sacrifice and death. Put your personal ambitions, life, strength, dreams, and plans on the altar and become a living sacrifice.

To carry revival fire, God's people must have faith–faith in God, faith in His Word, faith in the call, and faith in the message that has been burned into your soul. Faith to believe that the world is hungry and waiting to be brought to Christ. Faith to believe in the outpouring of the Holy Spirit and the rain from Heaven to fall in these last days when God is pouring out His Spirit upon all flesh. Faith to believe that if we preach the Word, the Lord is faithful to confirm it with signs following. Faith to believe that Jesus is in control, directing us, guiding us, and breaking through on our behalf. Faith to believe that God can bring revival out of the hardest, most impossible circumstances. Faith to believe that God can and will turn every attack of the enemy back into his own ranks to work his own defeat. Faith to believe that God is greater than the devil, keeping our eyes on the Author and Perfecter of our faith, never doubting for a moment that you are victorious in Him. Faith to laugh at defeat and obstacles and to see nothing but God's power and promises.

Revival fire doesn't cause you to look forward or around. It causes you to look up and be completely dependent on the Lord.

Every move of God comes with a price. It costs comfort. It definitely costs pride. And it will always cost control. Revival will expose idols and shake everything built on the flesh. But what God builds in the fire cannot be shaken. The early disciples knew something about this. They didn't have wealth, marketing, or buildings but they had fire and that fire spread through persecution until it turned the world upside down.

"These who have turned the world upside down have come here too."–Acts 17:6

Revival fire disrupts. It demands full surrender. It breaks pride and it exposes sin so that holiness and power can return to God's people. The deeper the repentance, the greater the power that follows.

THE CRY OF THIS GENERATION

The Church of Jesus Christ has a desperate need in this hour. It needs power. We don't need new trends or strategies. We need the truth of God's Word. We need a Church that carries the same fire that fell in the upper room. We need a Church that walks in Holy Ghost boldness again.

This is the call of revival fire–to awaken the sleeping, to reach the lost, to heal the sick, to equip the saints for battle, to enforce God's Kingdom, and to dismantle the kingdom of darkness. We are not waiting for revival, revival is waiting for us. The same Spirit that raised Christ from the dead lives in us. When we yield fully to Him, that all-consuming fire burns through us to reach the world.

> *"Will You not revive us again, that Your people may rejoice in You?"–Psalm 85:6*

Revival fire never stays inside the walls of the church. It overflows into the streets, into schools, and into cities until the moral fabric of society begins to change. Revival always produces evangelism–the unstoppable desire to tell others about Jesus. When the fire of God touches a person's life, they aren't able to stay silent about Jesus. They become a living testimony that Jesus is alive; not a dead, crucified, powerless Savior but a living, resurrected, omnipotent Savior. The soul that is revived will always be a soul-winner.

> *"But you shall receive power when the Holy Spirit has come upon you; and you shall be witnesses to Me in Jerusalem, and in all Judea and Samaria, and to the end of the earth."–Acts 1:8*

Evangelism is not optional for the Spirit-filled believer. It is the result of being on fire for God. When you've encountered His presence, you can't help but carry it to others. The early church preached Christ crucified and resurrected, and God confirmed their message with signs following.

> *"And they went out and preached everywhere, the Lord working with them and confirming the word through the accompanying signs."–Mark 16:20*

Miracles, signs, and wonders are not for just a few and they are not just for the pages of our bibles. They are the inheritance of every believer filled with the Spirit and they are for now. They are not for show, but for souls. Every healing, every deliverance, and every miracle testifies that Jesus is alive and still working through His Church today.

When the fire of revival falls, the lost are drawn to the power of God. Families are restored, addicts are set free, and entire regions feel the impact of Heaven on earth. Revival without outreach soon dies out. But revival with soul-winning becomes a force that cannot be stopped. We have received the same fire that fell at Pentecost and the fire of Pentecost has a purpose; that purpose is to receive power to be a witness for Jesus. The clock is ticking. Time is running out. It's the final call. It's time for every born again believer to take the message of Christ and the fire of God to the ends of the earth.

"Go therefore and make disciples of all the nations..."–Matthew 28:19

The outpouring of the Spirit in our generation is not meant to be contained within our churches. The fire of God that fills you also sends you and empowers you to heal the sick, cast out demons, and proclaim the death, burial, and resurrection of Jesus Christ with boldness. This is the fruit of revival–the demonstration of God's Kingdom in power.

Now is the time. The fire has already fallen. The Spirit has already been poured out. The only question is–will you carry it?

"Therefore go into the highways, and as many as you find, invite to the wedding."–Matthew 22:9

The call for revival fire is not just to be filled with fire, it's to go forth with fire to be a witness and a living carrier of Holy Ghost power to the ends of the earth.

Do you want to change your life? Burn for Jesus.

Do you want to change your family? Burn for Jesus.

Do you want to change your church? Burn for Jesus.

Do you want to change your city? Burn for Jesus.

Do you want to change the world? Burn for Jesus.

Burn with revival fire and change the world, or blend in and become a victim to its darkness.

TWO
HOLY GHOST POWER THAT SHAKES THE EARTH

"If you seek nothing but the will of God, He will always put you in His power and use you to shake the nations." –Smith Wigglesworth

Before tongues of fire rested on the heads of 120 believers in an upper room, the Holy Spirit was a promise spoken from the mouth of Jesus Himself. The baptism in the Holy Spirit was not an idea birthed by men. It was the Promise of the Father to empower every believer as a witness of Christ, in order that they might continue the ministry of Christ on the earth.

"Behold, I send the Promise of My Father upon you; but tarry in the city of Jerusalem until you are endued with power from on high."–Luke 24:49

The Father promised power. Jesus confirmed it. And the Church received it. The baptism in the Holy Spirit is Heaven's answer to human weakness. The same power that raised Christ from the dead not only dwells in, but fills, and overflows out of every born-again, blood-bought believer like rivers of living water.

This promise was not just for one generation or one culture. Peter declared on the day of Pentecost:

"For the promise is to you and to your children, and to all who are afar off, as many as the Lord our God will call."–Acts 2:39

The outpouring of the Holy Spirit was never meant to fade into history. It was meant to multiply and increase through every generation until the return of Christ. The early believers understood that the outpouring of the Holy Spirit was not a temporary experience but an all-consuming fire and presence that empowered them daily.

From the beginning, the Holy Spirit hovered over creation (Genesis 1:2). He filled craftsmen with skill in Moses' day, clothed Gideon with power, came upon David with anointing, and spoke through the prophets. But the Spirit didn't find His permanent dwelling in humanity until redemption was complete at Calvary's Cross.

At Calvary, the veil was torn so that Heaven could invade earth; not just in a temple made with hands, but within the hearts of believers. Jesus' resurrection made the human heart a new temple for the Holy Spirit's presence.

> *"Do you not know that you are the temple of God and that the Spirit of God dwells in you?"–1 Corinthians 3:16*

What a miracle! The same Spirit who empowered Jesus Christ's ministry now lives in us. The same Spirit who healed the sick through Jesus, who cast out devils, who raised Lazarus from the dead, and who anointed Him to preach good news to the poor–that same Spirit lives in you.

Jesus didn't ever want His followers to have to rely on human strength. He knew our strength would fail us. His command was not "Go and try," but "Wait and receive." He knew that without the power of the Holy Ghost, our abilities and passion would not be enough.

When the Holy Spirit came, Peter–the man who had denied Christ three times–stood up and preached with such authority that three thousand souls were saved. The Coward of Calvary became the Preaching Prophet of Pentecost. What changed? Not Peter's personality, but his power source.

The baptism in the Holy Spirit is not optional for the believer who wants to live a victorious life. It is Heaven's equipping for our assignment here on earth.

THE PURPOSE OF THE PROMISE

The Holy Spirit was not given just to make believers feel spiritual. It was given to make us effective. The presence of the Holy Spirit brings transformation within and the power of the Holy Spirit releases demonstration without.

When the Spirit fills a man or a woman, they become a vessel through which Jesus continues His work on the earth. The gospel moves from words to power.

> *"My speech and my preaching were not with persuasive words of human wisdom, but in demonstration of the Spirit and of power."*
> *–1 Corinthians 2:4*

The church was born in power, sustained by power, and is meant to finish in even greater power. The End-Time Church will not be weak and weary but victorious and full of the Holy Spirit and fire.

The Holy Spirit is God. He is the third Person of the Trinity, equal in power and nature with the Father and the Son. Many in the church acknowledge the existence of the Holy Spirit but they don't really know His personality. It's important to understand that revival is impossible without a relationship with the Holy Spirit. We are living in the dispensation of the Holy Spirit. He is God on earth right now. He is an all-powerful force. He is the Source of the fire we so desperately need. He is a Person and He can change anything and everything. When He is welcomed and His presence is honored, an atmosphere immediately shifts and becomes alive.

The Holy Spirit is not an "it." He is He. He has a will and He has intellect. He speaks, leads, comforts, teaches, and can be grieved. When you begin to understand Him as a Person, your walk with God becomes awakened with power. When you begin to understand Him as a Person, your prayer life shifts from obligation to relationship and church services shift from entertainment to encounter.

The most important ministry of the Holy Spirit is to glorify Jesus Christ. He draws attention away from Himself and points all glory to the Son. Every true move of the Spirit exalts Christ–not personalities, not programs, not emotions–but Jesus, the Lamb of God who takes away the sin of the world.

"He will glorify Me, for He will take of what is Mine and declare it to you."–John 16:14

When the Holy Spirit moves in power, people encounter Jesus Christ. Revival fire burns when Jesus is exalted at the center. The Holy Spirit reveals Him through preaching, prayer, prophecy, miracles, and the transformed lives of believers.

The Holy Spirit does not compete with the Word. He confirms it. The same Spirit who inspired Scripture still breathes on it when it's preached and read today. That's why dead religion comes alive when the Spirit breathes on the Word. It's the difference between information and revelation. The Holy Spirit marks the difference between learning about God and encountering Him.

The Holy Spirit is the believer's greatest Teacher. He makes truth come alive and gives understanding that human intellect cannot grasp. Every revelation and every insight comes through Him.

> *"But the Helper, the Holy Spirit, whom the Father will send in My name, He will teach you all things, and bring to your remembrance all things that I said to you."–John 14:26*

Without the Spirit's teaching, even the most educated Christian will remain powerless. Knowledge without revelation will often produce pride, but revelation through the Holy Spirit produces transformation.

The Holy Spirit not only teaches but leads. He is the inward Guide who directs believers.

> *"For as many as are led by the Spirit of God, these are sons of God."–Romans 8:14*

The Holy Spirit will always lead you closer to Jesus.

Jesus called the Holy Spirit "the Comforter" because He knew we would need His power and presence in a dark world. Jesus knew we would have trials but He gave us the Holy Spirit to strengthen us to overcome them. The Holy Spirit comforts us in the midst of brokenness. He restores us in the midst of weariness. He gives us peace in the midst of chaos. He is our Helper.

> *"And I will pray the Father, and He will give you another Helper, that He may abide with you forever."–John 14:16*

When Jesus walked the earth, He could only be in one place at a time. But through the Holy Spirit, His presence now fills the hearts and lives of millions simultaneously. That's why He said, "It is to your advantage that I go away." The Holy Spirit brings the presence of Jesus to live inside us as a living Person and salvation as a living reality.

There is no revival without the Holy Ghost. He is the atmosphere of Heaven on earth. When believers yield to His direction and honor His presence, His power flows freely. But when the Holy Spirit is ignored or resisted, the fire fades and His manifest Presence dissipates.

> *"Do not grieve the Holy Spirit of God, by whom you were sealed for the day of redemption."–Ephesians 4:30*

"Do not quench the Spirit."–1 Thessalonians 5:19

The more we honor the Holy Spirit, the more of His power we experience. He is waiting to be pursued, invited, obeyed, and trusted. Where hunger rises, His presence increases.

When Moses cried out, "If Your Presence does not go with us, do not bring us up from here," he was declaring the heartbeat of every true revivalist. Without the presence of the Holy Ghost, ministry becomes empty and mechanical. Without Him, preaching becomes powerless. Without His anointing, worship becomes entertainment.

The presence of the Holy Spirit distinguishes the Church from every other organization on earth. He makes us different. He makes us alive. When He fills a room, everything changes.

"Then the cloud covered the tabernacle of meeting, and the glory of the Lord filled the tabernacle."–Exodus 40:34

We are carriers of that same glory; His presence. We are moving temples of fire who can bring the atmosphere of Heaven into every situation.

THE BAPTISM IN THE HOLY SPIRIT

The Baptism of the Holy Spirit is a gift for every born again believer. The Baptism of the Holy Spirit is a separate experience from salvation. At salvation, you are *indwelt* with the

Holy Spirit. At the baptism in the Holy Spirit, you are *filled* with the Holy Spirit. People often say, "I have the Holy Spirit already because I am saved." And that is true, but the question is not whether you have the Holy Spirit. The question is, "Does the Holy Spirit have you?" The *baptism* in the Holy Spirit is an infilling presence beyond an indwelling presence. The baptism in the Holy Spirit is an encounter with God when you receive a gift, the Promise of the Father. You are submerged in a river of fire and out of you flows rivers of living water and heavenly tongues, a language that your natural mind does not create. However, like with any other gift, you must have a "yes" in your spirit to receive it.

The baptism in the Holy Spirit is an overflow of God's presence, in the life of a believer, that equips them to live and minister supernaturally.

"For John truly baptized with water, but you shall be baptized with the Holy Spirit not many days from now."–Acts 1:5

Water baptism is for repentance and identification with Christ as His follower. Holy Spirit baptism is for empowerment and demonstration of Christ as His follower One cleanses and the other commissions.

The day of Pentecost in Acts chapter 2 was not a one-time spiritual phenomenon. It was the model for every believer. Jesus had already breathed the Holy Spirit into His disciples for salvation in John 20:22, representing the indwelling presence of the Holy Spirit but in Acts chapter 2, they received power for ministry, representing the infilling presence of the Holy Spirit. Salvation gives you eternal life. Holy Spirit Baptism gives you power.

> *"When the Day of Pentecost had fully come, they were all with one accord in one place. And suddenly there came a sound from Heaven, as of a rushing mighty wind, and it filled the whole house where they were sitting. Then there appeared to them divided tongues, as of fire, and one sat upon each of them. And they were all filled with the Holy Spirit and began to speak with other tongues, as the Spirit gave them utterance."–Acts 2:1-4*

Revival fire– Pentecost fire– still falls today and the result is the same–boldness and supernatural power. Baptism in the Holy Ghost transforms ordinary men and women into witnesses of extraordinary power.

From the first outpouring, speaking in tongues accompanied the infilling of the Spirit. It is not the fullness of the experience but it is typically the first outward sign that the Holy Spirit has filled the surrendered vessel.

> *"For he who speaks in a tongue does not speak to men but to God, for no one understands him; however, in the spirit he speaks mysteries."–1 Corinthians 14:2*

Lester Sumrall often said, "The baptism in the Holy

Spirit is God taking hold of your whole being–spirit, soul, and body–to make you His instrument on the earth."

THE PURPOSE OF THE BAPTISM

The purpose of the baptism in the Holy Spirit is power for service. Jesus said, "You shall receive power... and you shall be witnesses." The Spirit fills believers so they can proclaim Christ with full authority and demonstrate His Kingdom through miracles, signs, and wonders.

The baptism in the Holy Spirit also ignites holiness. Fire empowers and it refines. The Holy Spirit empowers only what He can make holy and He transforms from the inside out. True Pentecostal power always walks hand in hand with holiness, character, and humility.

> *"He will baptize you with the Holy Spirit and fire."*–Matthew 3:11

Fire changes everything it touches. The believer baptized in the Holy Spirit becomes unrecognizable to the world–burning, filled with boldness, and consumed with a love for souls. The baptism in the Holy Spirit is not the end of spiritual pursuit. It is the beginning of a Spirit-filled life of power and miracles; the life of a witness who carries on the work of Jesus Christ on the earth.

There is one baptism but there are many refillings. The disciples who were filled in Acts chapter 2 were filled again in Acts chapter 4 when they faced persecution. The Holy Spirit's infilling is meant to be continuous, not occasional.

> *"And when they had prayed, the place where they were assembled together was shaken; and they were all filled with the Holy Spirit, and they spoke the word of God with boldness."–Acts 4:31*

Spirit-filled believers must stay under the flow of God's power. The believer who continually yields to the Holy Spirit will remains full, effective, and on fire. The key is daily surrender and sacrifice–allowing the Holy Spirit to direct every step of your life and consume every area of your life. .

The measure to which we yield is the measure to which He will fill. A life half-surrendered will never walk in full power, but the believer who lives completely yielded to the Holy Spirit will overflow everywhere they go.

When the Holy Spirit fills people, the result is expansion. It is God's supreme will to win the lost and expand His Kingdom until Christ's return. Missionaries are sent. Evangelists are raised up. The supernatural becomes natural. Baptism in the Holy Ghost fuels soul winning and confirms the gospel through demonstration power.

> *"Our gospel did not come to you in word only, but also in power, and in the Holy Spirit and in much assurance."–1 Thessalonians 1:5*

This is why revival fire leads back to Pentecost. There is no revival without the Holy Spirit and fire. The Holy Ghost is not an optional add on to Christianity. He is the breath, life, and power of the Church. With Him and Him alone, a spiritual invasion of Heaven on Earth can occur.

The baptism in the Holy Spirit was given first, and primarily, for public empowerment. The first evidence of Pentecost was disciples, who once hid in fear, stepped into the streets of Jerusalem declaring the name of Jesus with supernatural boldness.

> *"But you shall receive power when the Holy Spirit has come upon you; and you shall be witnesses to Me in Jerusalem, and in all Judea and Samaria, and to the end of the earth."–Acts 1:8*

The word "power" in this verse is dunamis–inherent power, strength, ability, miraculous force, explosive power that produces change; miracle-working power. It's where we get the word "dynamite." When the Holy Ghost fills a believer, that believer is filled with power from another world in order that they would change this world.

The Holy Spirit transforms cowards into conquerors and spectators into soul-winners. A church without power hides behind walls but a church full of the Holy Ghost charges the gates of hell.

"For God has not given us a spirit of fear, but of power and of love and of a sound mind."–2 Timothy 1:7

The world we are living in pushes a doctrine of fear that only the fire of God can consume. And fear is not broken by determination–it is broken by the fire of the Holy Ghost. When the Holy Spirit fills you, timidity dies and boldness rises. You stop asking, "What will they think?" and start asking, "Who will be saved?"

The early Church didn't preach with clever words but with Holy Ghost power. The Holy Spirit took ordinary fishermen and made them prophetic voices that pierced the hearts of men.

Revival preaching is not about eloquence. It's about Holy Ghost anointing. Revival preaching is not easy to swallow. It provokes and it irritates religion. It offends complacency and it awakens those who are "at ease in Zion." Revival preaching causes a person to run to Jesus or to walk away from the church mad because it demands a decision. Either pick up your cross and follow Jesus or find another church to make excuses. Lukewarm Christians will not be comfortable in atmospheres where revival preaching is the norm, but hungry, yielded Christians will be empowered and their fire will burn brighter. Revival preaching is gasoline on the hearts of the burning and it contains the anointing necessary to penetrate the hearts of the lost unto salvation.

When the Spirit anoints a message, conviction follows.

It's not just heard–it's felt. Words become weapons of truth that cut through deception and awaken souls to repentance. Every time the gospel is preached under the anointing, chains are broken. Demons will flee and souls will be eternally saved. Without that power, preaching becomes a history lesson, a show, a performance or some good advice. But with it, preaching becomes an encounter with the living God.

Jesus didn't just preach about the Kingdom–He demonstrated it. The purpose of Pentecostal power is not to impress people. The purpose of Pentecostal power is to impact lost souls and change the world.

"How God anointed Jesus of Nazareth with the Holy Spirit and with power, who went about doing good and healing all who were oppressed by the devil, for God was with Him."–Acts 10:38

When revival fire is burning in someone's life, miracles will follow. Power is proof that Jesus is alive. Miracles, signs, and wonders are not extra–they are evidence of Jesus. The Book of Acts is not a history book; it is a blueprint for Spirit-filled living.

The apostle Paul declared:

"For the Kingdom of God is not in word but in power." –1 Corinthians 4:20

Every believer is called to demonstrate that power. You may never stand behind a pulpit, but you can tell people boldly about the death, burial, and resurrection of Jesus Christ–lay hands on the sick, cast out demons, and speak life to the broken. The power to witness is not limited to preachers–it belongs to the Church. It belongs to you.

THE FIRE THAT SPREADS

The early Church grew because its members preached everywhere they went. Revival spreads when believers move from the pews to the streets. When believers move in Holy Ghost power, that power pours out everywhere the gospel is preached.

> *"Therefore those who were scattered went everywhere preaching the word."*–Acts 8:4

Revival begins with a few who carry the fire of God until it consumes a city. The same fire that fell in Jerusalem must now burn in Los Angeles, New York, Tijuana, Soyapango, Nairobi, and every corner of the earth.

This is the New Testament pattern–Word and Spirit colliding together. When the message and the demonstration unite, revival explodes. It's not either/or–it's both/and. The power to witness is the power to demonstrate. The power to demonstrate is the power to change lives. The gospel of Jesus Christ is unstoppable when it's carried by fire and power.

The Spirit of God tore the veil after Jesus' death and turned fearfilled disciples into unbreakable warriors. That same power and fire is burning in your heart right now. We are in a battle. It's an ancient battle. It rages all around us. It's the battle for the souls of mankind and you are not a bystander in this war–you are a weapon in the hands of Almighty God and He has given you the power you need.

God's power isn't weak. You were not saved to just sit on a church pew. You were saved to confront darkness, to heal the broken, to cast down strongholds, and to declare war on sin and death. When the power of God flows through you, fear loses its grip, depression breaks, addiction bends, souls are saved, and cities change. Because where the power of God is released, the fire spreads.

Don't live tame when you carry power. Don't settle for safety when resurrection power lives inside you. It's time for believers to shake everything that can be shaken with the power of God.

God is looking for men and women who will stand as vessels of unstoppable power–not perfect vessels, but vessels who are plugged into His power and therefore dangerous to hell. Let the Holy Spirit take your life and use it until it breaks through all the darkness around you. Let Him shake everything that can be shaken until only His kingdom remains. (Hebrews 12:27)

This is Holy Ghost power that shakes the earth–it's not born of man and it's not weak. It's the living force of the Holy Spirit of God; power from another world, moving through flesh and blood, to change this world.

You've been entrusted with that power. And the order still stands:

"Go in the power of the Spirit."

THREE
HOLY GHOST FIRE THAT DEVOURS DARKNESS

"The old spirit, the old fire that once burned in the midst of the saints of God, is there still, but it burns very low at present. We want—I cannot say how much—we want a revival of pure and undefiled religion in this our day. Will it come? Why should it not come? If we long for it, if we pray for it, if we believe for it, if we work for it, and prepare for it, it will certainly come. The day will break, and the shadows will flee away." –Charles H Spurgeon

Spurgeon saw clearly and spoke cuttingly. I dare to say. The day is breaking and the shadows are fleeing away.

Darkness doesn't hide anymore and the Church shouldn't either.

Darkness isn't passive. Darkness advertises and it strategizes. It parades in the streets, it sells itself on screens, and it has trained a generation to laugh at and mock all that is good and Godly.

Darkness has shaped ideologies, fueled corruption, glamorized rebellion, and packaged sin in a cute little box. The dark forces that opposed the prophets and crucified Christ are whispering through every godless system today. Paul called them *"principalities, powers, the rulers of the darkness of this age"* (Ephesians 6:12). They have changed their camouflage, but not their mission.

Look around. Deception has become a brand, lust has become a lucrative industry, and pride has become a badge of success. Families are being broken into pieces and culture calls it progress. Life changing gospel truth has been traded for tolerance. Conviction is mocked as hate and holiness is laughed at as outdated. The spirit of Babylon has gone digital, and it is discipling nations through screens. That serpent, the devil, that lied to Eve now slithers through algorithms, tempting hearts to call darkness light, and to call evil good.

There remains only one cure; one strategy: The light of Jesus shines in the darkness and the darkness cannot overcome it (John 1:5). The fire of God does not negotiate with darkness–it was designed to devour it.

From the beginning, the first words of creation split the void as darkness was over the deep: *"Let there be light"* and the dominion of darkness was shattered. The Light, that the darkness cannot overcome, now burns in the believer. Jesus said, *"I am the light of the world,"* and then turned to His followers and said, *"You are the light of the world."*

When Elijah stood on Mount Carmel, he didn't debate Baal. He called down fire. When the upper room filled with 120 disciples, they didn't blend into the crowd, they burned so much that the crowd could not ignore the fire; resulting in three thousand souls being saved. Every time light collides with darkness, the darkness can not overcome it.

The Holy Spirit and fire move through yielded vessels. He sets men on fire to confront lies and deception with truth. The darkness of this generation is loud, but the fire of God is louder. It confronts and pulls down strongholds that politics can't touch. The fire of God breaks addictions that talking on therapy couches can't fix, and it melts hard hearts that religion can't reach.

You can curse the darkness all you want. But I suggest you carry the flame that devours it. Devouring the darkness around us begins with each of us, individually, being willing, and desperate enough to be consumed by the fire of God.

THE NATURE OF GOD'S FIRE

Revival fire is more than excitement. It is the nature of God Himself. When God reveals Himself, His presence burns like fire. His fire refines what is clean and consumes what is unholy.

"For our God is a consuming fire."–Hebrews 12:29

Before fire empowers, it consumes and refines. Before God uses a person publicly, He refines them privately. The modern believer often prays for power, but God answers with fire. Power will destroy what fire has not yet cleansed. He doesn't pour new oil into old wineskins. Before He sends revival through us, He sends fire to us–to refine our motives, cleanse our hearts, and separate flesh from Spirit.

When the fire of the Holy Spirit burns, it exposes what has been hidden beneath the surface. Sin, pride, and compromise cannot survive in His presence. The closer we draw to Him, the more clearly we see ourselves. This is not condemnation–it is transformation.

Every great revival and awakening began privately before it became public. Evan Roberts of the Welsh Revival prayed for years before the fire spread. The Azusa Street Revival was born out of a small prayer meeting led by hungry believers in Los Angeles. The Spirit still works the same way–He revives individuals before He revives nations.

You can't bring revival to others until you've experienced it yourself. Personal revival is all about pursuit. It's choosing to stay on fire when others grow cold, to stay humble when others want recognition, and to stay hungry when others grow comfortable.

When one person burns for Jesus and refuses to let that fire go out, others around them catch fire too.

THE PATH TO PERSONAL REVIVAL

Isaiah encountered this kind of fire when he saw the Lord high and lifted up. The glory of God convicted him. Let me explain it like this: When you encounter and get close to the holiness of God, the glory of God; it is not a comfortable place. It's a fearful place. It's a place that exposes everything ugly in you, the hidden places, the sin, the thoughts you shouldn't have, the jealousy, the hatred, the bitterness, the fear, the anger, the insecurity, the pride, the comparison, the sinful nature, the flesh nature, the selfish nature, the wickedness, the dryness, the rebellion, the complacency, the worldliness, your indifference to a dying world, your coldness, and more.

The holiness of God should cause you like Isaiah to cry out "Woe is me, for I am undone."

> "Then I said, 'Woe is me, for I am undone! Because I am a man of unclean lips, and I dwell in the midst of a people of unclean lips; for my eyes have seen the King, the Lord of hosts.'"–Isaiah 6:5

Only after Isaiah confessed his uncleanness did the fire touch his lips and cleanse him. The same process still happens today–God's fire reveals so that it can heal. His conviction is not rejection; it's an invitation to become more like Him. It's an invitation to personally burn with the fires of revival.

> *"In the year that King Uzziah died, I saw the Lord sitting on a throne, high and lifted up, and the train of His robe filled the temple. Above it stood seraphim; each one had six wings: with two he covered his face, with two he covered his feet, and with two he flew. And one cried to another and said: "Holy, holy, holy is the LORD of hosts; The whole earth is full of His glory!" And the posts of the door were shaken by the voice of him who cried out, and the house was filled with smoke. So I said: "Woe is me, for I am undone! Because I am a man of unclean lips, And I dwell in the midst of a people of unclean lips; For my eyes have seen the King, The LORD of hosts." Then one of the seraphim flew to me, having in his hand a live coal which he had taken with the tongs from the altar. And he touched my mouth with it, and said: "Behold, this has touched your lips; Your iniquity is taken away, And your sin purged." Also I heard the voice of the Lord, saying: "Whom shall I send, And who will go for Us?" Then I said, "Here am I! Send me." And He said, "Go and tell this people..."–Isaiah 6:1-9*

The background of this portion of scripture gives us a foundation that is necessary to understand the role of the fire of God's presence in pursuit of personal revival.

King Uzziah, like many, thought he could do what he liked in the temple of God. He is a prime example of someone that handled adversity better than success. As long as he sought the Lord God made him prosper, but in his success, he became proud in his heart and sinned against God. He entered the temple of the Lord to burn incense, where no king was to go. Eighty one priests withstood him but in his anger, pride, and disobedience, God struck him with leprosy and he was an isolated leper until he died. Eighty one priests withstood him but we read of only one who sought the Lord. The throne of Israel was empty. But Isaiah sought God, whose throne is never empty. Someone had to break through with God. Isaiah did.

So King Uzziah is dead and there's an empty throne. Where was the Lord in all this? The Lord was sitting on His throne. God was still enthroned in Heaven and was still in charge of all creation. There is still a throne in Heaven, and the Lord God sits upon it as the sovereign ruler of the universe. This is a fact. There is an occupied throne in Heaven. It's not a chair. It's a throne. And regardless of the wickedness and darkness in this world, God is still sovereign and reigning in full power. Whatever we face in this world and whatever we face in this nation, God Almighty reigns. God is still on the throne. He is the Lord strong & mighty. He is the Lord mighty in battle.

> *(verse 5)* *"So I said: "Woe is me, for I am undone! Because I am a man of unclean lips, and I dwell in the midst of a people of unclean lips; For my eyes have seen the King, The* Lord *of hosts."*

Isaiah saw himself as he really was. Now he is where all personal revivals start-with repentance. The great Charles Spurgeon said "undone" carries with it the thought of being pulled to pieces to the point of destruction.

In this portion of scripture Isaiah is no longer trying to get his spirituality from somebody else or protecting his prophetic reputation. This preacher is saying, "This most consecrated, trained part of me, is unclean." This is what the presence of a holy God does. Even the most sanctified among us fall to our knees in the fire of God's presence crying out, "Woe is me."

> *(verse 6-7) "Then one of the seraphim flew to me, having in his hand a live coal which he had taken with the tongs from the altar. And he touched my mouth with it, and said: "Behold, this has touched your lips; Your iniquity is taken away, and your sin purged."*

Isaiah's mouth got burnt. If you are going to bless, if you are going to preach, if you are going to pray effectively, if you are going to be a voice for God in this generation, you first have to burn.

Isaiah had a vision of the holiness of God, his own sinfulness, and God's ability to cleanse him. Then he saw the need around him. And now he can lead in repentance, power, "undoneness," and in seeking the face of God.

The secret of personal revival is radical obedience out of a clean heart.

Now, and only now...

(verse 8) "Also I heard the voice of the Lord, saying: "Whom shall I send, and who will go for Us?" Then I said, "Here am I! Send me."

The world is full of noise. We hear echoes, opinions, and the plans of men.

Isaiah heard God's voice because he was clean. *"Who will go for us?"*

There is no hesitation in a burning heart. "Send me."

(Verse 9) And He said, "Go and tell this people...

The Lord said "Go."

Do you want to be sent? Do you want to be a mouthpiece for God? Do you want to be used by God as a burning flame that devours the darkness around you?

If you do, then you have to get close to a holy God; close enough to be changed and lit on fire by His holy presence.

"Who may ascend into the hill of the Lord? Or who may stand in His holy place?"–Psalm 24:3

Duncan Campbell, used of God in the Hebrides Revival

of the 1950s, was preaching one night when the Heavens seemed like brass. Duncan stopped preaching, and he called on a young man to pray. The boy stopped before he prayed and said, "What's the use of praying if we are not right with God?" He then recited the 24th Psalm.

> *The earth is the LORD's, and all its fullness, The world and those who dwell therein. For He has founded it upon the seas, And established it upon the waters. <u>Who may ascend into the hill of the LORD? Or who may stand in His holy place? He who has clean hands and a pure heart, Who has not lifted up his soul to an idol, Nor sworn deceitfully.</u> He shall receive blessing from the LORD, And righteousness from the God of his salvation. This is Jacob, the generation of those who seek HimWho seek Your face. Lift up your heads, O you gates! And be lifted up, you everlasting doors! And the King of glory shall come in. Who is this King of glory? The LORD strong and mighty, The LORD mighty in battle. Lift up your heads, O you gates! Lift up, you everlasting doors! And the King of glory shall come in. Who is this King of glory? The LORD of hosts, He is the King of glory. -Psalm 24*

The fear of the Lord came upon them. The fire of God fell and the area knew that the Lord had visited His people.

The Lord is demanding in this 24th Psalm. God says we cannot "ascend the hill of the Lord" (come into His holy presence) in an unholy state. *"Who shall stand in his holy place?"*

God gives the answer: *"He who has clean hands and a pure heart"* (Ps. 24:4).

How close do you want to be to God? Will you ascend the hill of the Lord? Are your hands clean? Is your heart pure? You're the one who is setting the distance to how close you can get to a holy God.

And I hear the Lord calling to His people, *"Come up here, be washed in the blood of Jesus, be cleansed, turn from your wicked ways and ascend the hill of the Lord; stand in My holy presence so I can light you on fire and fill you with power."*

Abandon whatever you have to abandon to ascend the hill of the Lord. Alter your life however you need to in order that your hands will remain clean and your heart will remain pure, to ascend the hill of the Lord.

He's calling you to more. He's calling you to an encounter in the Spirit beyond where you are right now. He's calling you to a place of freedom.

He's calling you to a place of presence. He's calling you to a place of glory.

He's calling you to a place of holiness. He's calling you to a place of burning. He's calling you to a place of personal revival.

THE FIRE OF HIS PRESENCE

When the Holy Spirit fills a room, His presence is not always comfortable. The presence of God is as much the Spirit of holiness as He is the Spirit of power.

The Holy Spirit doesn't just rest on the pure–He purifies those He rests on. When revival fire comes, hearts are exposed. Hypocrisy is uncovered. Secret sin is revealed. Not to shame, but to set free. The consuming fire of God removes everything that keeps His people from walking in the fullness of God.

Throughout Scripture, fire symbolizes God's method of separating the genuine from the counterfeit. Gold is refined in fire because only heat can separate the pure from the impure. In the same way, God uses trials, testing, and conviction to refine His people.

> *"But He knows the way that I take; when He has tested me, I shall come forth as gold."–Job 23:10*

We often ask God to increase our anointing, but He first increases the heat. The refining fire is proof that God is preparing you for more. Revival does not come through comfortable believers–it comes through crucified ones. To walk in revival fire means to let God burn away everything that doesn't look like Jesus.

Fire attracts. People are drawn to the believer who burns with holy fire. But that same fire that attracts the hungry repels the religious. Revival fire will also divide–it separates those who want God from those content with religion.

Just as God called Moses from a burning bush, God still calls from the fire. When a believer is fully surrendered, their life becomes an altar. The moment a believer cries out for more of God, Heaven responds with fire–but not always the kind of fire they expect. God's refining fire strengthens and develops us. He refines His people as gold in the furnace, removing the impurities that weaken, and hinder our relationship with Him.

> *"Behold, I have refined you, but not as silver; I have tested you in the furnace of affliction."–Isaiah 48:10*

The refining process is the hidden work of revival. God does not anoint what He has not refined. He allows the pressure of trials, the heat of correction, and the fire of His presence to prepare His people for greater glory.

Heat exposes what is hidden. Revival fire always begins with exposure. The Holy Spirit both fills and reveals. This process makes room for greater power.

> *"He will sit as a refiner and a purifier of silver; He will purify the sons of Levi, and purge them as gold and silver, that they may offer to the Lord an offering in righteousness."–Malachi 3:3*

The refiner doesn't walk away from the furnace. He stays near, watching the gold carefully. He knows the process is complete when He can see His reflection in it. God's goal for your life is the same–He will keep refining until you reflect the image of Christ.

Every revival generation goes through refining before rising. God is not punishing His people–He's purifying them for a greater outpouring. The shaking in the Church of Jesus Christ has not been a sign of God's absence but of His preparation. He is separating the pure from the impure and the hungry from the satisfied.

The fire is falling again–not just to empower but to refine. Those who yield to this process will carry lasting revival. Those who resist it will watch it pass them by.

"Therefore thus says the Lord of hosts: Behold, I will refine them and try them; for how shall I deal with the daughter of My people?"–Jeremiah 9:7

When God refines, what was ordinary and common becomes miraculous and extraordinary.

THE ALTAR OF SURRENDER

Throughout Scripture, it is clear that God sent His fire where there was a sacrifice. The altar is the meeting place between Heaven and earth, the place where flesh dies and the Spirit reigns.

The greater the fire you desire, the greater the surrender

required. The measure of fire on your life will match the measure of surrender in your heart.

> *"I beseech you therefore, brethren, by the mercies of God, that you present your bodies a living sacrifice, holy, acceptable to God, which is your reasonable service."*–Romans 12:1

The world measures greatness by how much you gain but the Kingdom of God measures it by how much you give. Revival fire does not fall on the proud or the comfortable. It falls on those who lay everything down on the altar of God.

The altar is not a place for negotiation, it's not a place for complaining, or for sharing your opinions with God–it's a place for death. You cannot keep your life and carry His fire. Jesus said plainly:

> *"If anyone desires to come after Me, let him deny himself, and take up his cross daily, and follow Me."*–Luke 9:23

Many pray for fire but resist The Cross that precedes it. The Cross is the altar of the New Covenant. It's where self dies so that the Holy Spirit can live fully through you. The flesh must be crucified before the fire can be sustained in your life.

Revival is costly because surrender is costly. Every idol, every ambition, every comfort that competes with Christ must go on the altar. When the fire falls, it consumes everything that isn't eternal.

The altar of surrender is built through worship. Worship is not a song; it's a sacrifice. True worship costs you something. It is laying your will on the altar. Jesus' prayer at Gethsemane, that preceded The Cross, was an agonizing exchange and it is our pathway to a crucified Christian life: *"Not my will, but Yours be done."* That is true worship.

When Solomon dedicated the temple, it wasn't the gold or the music that drew the fire–it was the sacrifice.

> *"When Solomon had finished praying, fire came down from Heaven and consumed the burnt offering and the sacrifices; and the glory of the Lord filled the temple."–2 Chronicles 7:1*

Worship that costs nothing changes nothing.

Under the New Covenant, we no longer build altars of stone–we become the altar. The fire of the Holy Spirit burns within the believer. You are the temple, and your life is the offering.

> *"Do you not know that your body is the temple of the Holy Spirit who is in you, whom you have from God, and you are not your own? For you were bought at a price; therefore glorify God in your body and in your spirit, which are God's."–1 Corinthians 6:19–20*

Surrender is not a one-time event. It's a daily altar and revival fire burns continuously in hearts that remain yielded and sacrificial. The more you surrender, the stronger the flame grows.

Every day you decide whether the fire increases or fades.

Elijah's story on Mount Carmel remains one of the greatest revival moments in Scripture. Surrounded by compromise, intimidation, and idolatry, he rebuilt the altar and called on the Lord. God answered with fire.

"Hear me, O Lord, hear me, that this people may know that You are the Lord God. Then the fire of the Lord fell and consumed the burnt sacrifice, and the wood and the stones and the dust, and it licked up the water that was in the trench."–1 Kings 18:37–38

Elijah rebuilt the altar before calling for the fire. Revival begins the same way–not with a platform, but with an altar. Before the fire of God consumes a church or a city or a generation, it first consumes people who are fully surrendered.

When the fire fell, the people fell too. They fell face down in repentance and awe. That's what revival looks like. When you surrender completely, you won't have to beg for fire–it will fall.

HOLINESS AND POWER

In God's Kingdom, power flows through holiness. Holiness is not a barrier to the anointing; it's the channel it flows through. Revival that lacks holiness burns fast and fades. Revival rooted in holiness endures and transforms generations and regions.

Holiness is not legalism; it's freedom. It's not bondage and rules. It's walking right before God. Holiness is not about perfection–it's about separation. To be holy means to be set apart for God's purposes and yielded to His will.

> *"As He who called you is holy, you also be holy in all your conduct, because it is written, 'Be holy, for I am holy.'"–1 Peter 1:15–16*

We are made holy through Christ's blood, but we walk in holiness by the Holy Spirit's power. The Cross makes us holy and the fire of God keeps us holy. One is instant and the other is continual. When your heart burns for Jesus, sin loses its attraction. Your appetites change. You hunger for the things of God more than the things of this world; and as you feast on good and godly things, what used to fulfill and satisfy you simply loses its taste.

> *"Blessed are the pure in heart, for they shall see God."–Matthew 5:8*

Walking holy and close to God is the path to walking in power. The devil tries to make holiness look restrictive because he knows it's the source of true power and freedom for believers. The holier you walk, the freer you become.

Holiness invites the presence of God because it is His nature. It's what Heaven looks like. When believers pursue holiness, they begin to live as citizens of Heaven on earth. The world sees the difference and is drawn to Jesus. Holiness doesn't push people away–it draws them in, because it reveals God.

There is a direct link between holiness and authority. The authority of a believer does not come from titles or charisma–it comes from a life holy before God. Jesus walked in absolute authority because He walked in absolute obedience.

"For the ruler of this world is coming, and he has nothing in Me."–John 14:30

When the enemy has nothing in you, he has no power over you. Sin gives Satan access but holiness shuts the door. That's why the Spirit calls believers to live undefiled. Believers need to walk in victory over the enemy, not in vulnerability to him.

Revivalists throughout history understood this: private consecration produces public power. Those who guard the secret place will carry fire in the public place.

The true evidence of revival is not what happens in a moment–it's how we live afterward. The refining fire must turn into a lifestyle that pleases God. Holiness that's sustained daily becomes the fuel that keeps the fire alive.

"Finally, then, brethren, we urge and exhort in the Lord Jesus that you should abound more and more, just as you received from us how you ought to walk and to please God."–1 Thessalonians 4:1

To please God means to live in continual agreement with His Spirit. Obedience is the pathway to power. The Spirit leads, but it's our obedience that keeps His fire flowing. Every act of obedience adds wood to the altar and every act of compromise removes it.

"If you love Me, keep My commandments."–John 14:15

God entrusts greater anointing to those who obey quickly. Delayed obedience is just disobedience in slow motion. Let me put it another way: delayed obedience is still disobedience. When you live to please God, obedience becomes natural. The more you obey, the more He trusts you with His presence and power. The fire of God burns on the altars of sacrifice and obedience.

When individuals burn, an entire church can become a

furnace of revival. The fire that purifies one believer can ignite a whole congregation–and when a church burns with holy fire, cities and regions are impacted and changed.

> *"Then the fire of the Lord fell, and the glory of the Lord filled the house."–2 Chronicles 7:1*

When the people of God burn, the presence of God manifests with undeniable force. The fire is preparing the Bride for the Bridegroom. Jesus is returning for a holy, spotless, and victorious Church.

> *"That He might present her to Himself a glorious church, not having spot or wrinkle or any such thing, but that she should be holy and without blemish."–Ephesians 5:27*

The end-time Church will not retreat in fear as the world grows darker. It will advance in power. The final move of God will be marked by a Bride full of power, clothed in righteousness, and burning for Jesus.

FIRE THAT DEVOURS DARKNESS

There is a holy war raging in this generation. The battle is not fought with swords and guns, but with fire–God's fire. Hell has unleashed a storm of wickedness and corruption.

Darkness calls itself light. Evil disguises itself as truth. But the fire of God is rising again–violent, effective and untamed. It does not negotiate. It consumes.

In Acts 28, Paul stood by a fire that drove out a viper. Wherever the true fire burns, serpents will always try to strike. But the fire will expose them and the power of God will shake them off. The Holy Spirit preserved Paul and He who burns in you can preserve you too. That fire makes you untouchable to the forces of darkness when you walk in obedience.

The prophet Nahum said, *"The mountains quake before Him, the hills melt, and the earth heaves at His presence"* (Nahum 1:5). When God's presence fills a man or a woman, you carry the power to make hell tremble. Every stronghold, every lie, and every demonic structure dismantles under the heat of His fire.

It's time for every born-again, blood-bought believer of Jesus Christ to burn again. The hour demands believers who have been refined by revival fire–men and women who refuse to compromise, who won't back down, and who speak with authority. The fire of God is the difference between a powerless church and a victorious one.

The fire that devours darkness is igniting hearts again. It burns away fear, shame, sin, mixture, and complacency. It fuels courage, boldness, power, dominion, truth, and holiness.

The battle lines are drawn. It is clear there is darkness all around us that needs to be devoured by the fire of God and the Spirit of the Lord is igniting His people to devour it. Step into the fire. Let it cleanse you, consume you, and then commission you.

Because when the fire of God moves through a yielded vessel–darkness doesn't stand a chance. It will be devoured.

FOUR
HEAVEN'S INVASION HAS BEGUN

"Give me one hundred preachers who fear nothing but sin and desire nothing but God, and I care not a straw whether they be clergymen or laymen; such alone will shake the gates of hell and set up the kingdom of Heaven on earth." –John Wesley

Revival is not a story we study–it's a fire we experience and there is no revival without fire. God has not changed. His passion for souls and His hunger to dwell among His people, in fire and Holy Ghost power, remain the same. The fire that fell in Jerusalem, Wales, and Azusa Street still burns for anyone hungry enough to receive it.

"Jesus Christ is the same yesterday, today, and forever."–Hebrews 13:8

Every generation has the opportunity to encounter God's revival fire and Heaven's invasion has begun in this generation.

Sadly, at some point, the Church gave the future of this world to experts, to education, to science, to politicians, and to culture–and they have all failed miserably. It's time for the Church of Jesus Christ to take back the future. The world is racing toward judgment, and the future is now.

We are currently living in a post-Christian world. So what should be our perspective as Christians, as those who claim to be bible believing? How should we look at this post-Christian, broken, and lost world? We must once again look at it through a bloody cross. We must once again look at it through an empty tomb. We must once again look at it through an upper room. We must once again look at it through the eyes of the persecuted and scattered early Church. We must once again look at it through the burning eyes of Jesus Christ–the Lion and the Lamb, the First and the Last, the Alpha and the Omega, the Beginning and the End, the Resurrection and the Life, the Great High Priest and the Intercessor, the Redeemer and the Deliverer, the King of kings and the Lord of lords, the Lamb who was slain, the Firstborn from the dead, the One who descended, snatched the keys of death, hell, and the grave from our adversary the devil, and then ascended and sat down at the right hand of the Father; Jesus, the Baptizer in Fire–Jesus, the Bridegroom who is coming back for His Bride.

If we, the Church, are going to influence and change this world, we need revival fire and we need a revolution. Revival is the act of the Spirit upon believers who have lost their first love. Revival is the Spirit's passion within the believer to know and obey the total will of God. Revival produces a willingness within the believer to forsake all–that God might be all in all. Revival is not a luxury or a marketing tool but a necessity; a fire that will overflow from our lives and invade this wicked, dark world with a Holy Ghost revolution. Thank God, revival is here and revival is now!

A revolution is a forcible overthrow of a government or social order in favor of a new system. That is what Jesus did. Heaven invaded earth. Jesus invaded and overthrew the religious systems of His day. He overthrew the cultural systems of His day. What makes you think He is somehow unable or unwilling to do that in our day? Jesus told His disciples it was better that He go, so the Holy Spirit could come. We need a Holy Ghost revolution of epic proportion in this world.

We are living in a day that is darker and more blatantly and unashamedly wicked than the days of Sodom and the days of Noah combined. If you are a Christian with even an ounce of spiritual discernment, you have no doubt that this generation needs a moral and spiritual revolution. And if that's true, the problem is that most individual believers do not think it is their responsibility to do anything about it–but it is.

God-transformed people transform churches, and the

Church of Jesus Christ will transform the world. Heaven is invading this world, through the Church. And the task of getting it cleansed is not easy, but it is also not impossible. Our only hope is a crucified, burning Church filled with crucified, burning believers.

> *"I have been crucified with Christ; it is no longer I who live, but Christ lives in me; and the life which I now live in the flesh I live by faith in the Son of God, who loved me and gave Himself for me."–Galatians 2:20*

What we need is another visit to The Cross. This time to get on it and be crucified with Christ, then a stop at the upper room for a fresh enduement of Pentecostal power.

The Spirit of God is calling His Church to make revival history not just to remember and admire it. The question is no longer "Will God move again?" but, "Will we make room for Him to move in us now?"

The average believer when confronted with the question "Do you want revival in our day?" will usually say, "Yes," but then walk out of the church doors and go back to life as usual. They are too busy for God. Too busy with work and family and scrolling on their phones to make room for revival. There is too much content, too much on the calendar, too much of the world, and too much entertainment competing with God for their time and attention. There is no sacrifice, no fasting, no feasting on the Word of God, no praying, and no hunger for the presence of God. Jesus, the Reviver, is our only hope. Make room for God and He will come.

Revival is not man's invention. It is not some idea that was dreamed up in a board room. Revival is an outpouring of the Holy Spirit and fire that began in an upper room. It is Heaven's invasion on earth. It's what happens when God's presence and glory is revealed in such a real way that sin loses its appeal, flesh no longer rules, all that competes with God's presence ceases to satisfy, and people turn wholeheartedly to Jesus. Revival is when God shows up in power among His people.

> *"Oh, that You would rend the Heavens! That You would come down! That the mountains might shake at Your presence."–Isaiah 64:1*

Every true revival has one central focus–the presence of God.

REVIVAL HAS NEVER ENDED

God's fire has never gone out–but it has moved from heart to heart, from nation to nation, and from generation to generation. The Holy Spirit has been igniting fires of revival and awakening across the globe, and they continue even now.

The Welsh Revival shook an entire nation in the early

1900s; the Azusa Street Revival sent missionaries worldwide; the Argentine and African outpourings in the late twentieth century stirred multitudes to repentance. But all of these were not endings–they were waves of one great flood of fire.

> *"For the earth will be filled with the knowledge of the glory of the Lord, as the waters cover the sea."–Habakkuk 2:14*

We are part of that same move today. Revival is not limited to a place or a name–it's constantly spreading through surrendered people everywhere. The Spirit of God is stirring homes, churches, and cities with fresh hunger. What we're seeing around the world is not a new thing–it's a continuation of Pentecost.

In our time, the Holy Spirit is once again calling believers to rebuild altars of prayer and sacrifice. Across nations, spontaneous worship gatherings, water baptisms, prayer movements, and evangelistic crusades are sparking fresh flames of revival. It's not confined to one denomination, race, or region–the fire is falling wherever people humble themselves and hunger for Him.

> *"For where two or three are gathered together in My name, I am there in the midst of them."–Matthew 18:20*

This is the hour of the outpouring. The Spirit is awakening young and old alike. He is restoring their first love. He is reigniting prayer and He is renewing a passion for souls. The fire that birthed the early Church is birthing a final harvest generation.

We are not waiting for revival–we are living in it. The question is not whether God will pour out His Spirit. He already has. The question is whether His people will be filled. The hungry will always be filled.

"Blessed are those who hunger and thirst for righteousness, for they shall be filled."–Matthew 5:6

The Spirit of God is looking for modern-day upper rooms–homes, hearts, and churches that will say, "Lord, do it again–here, now, and in us." Revival fire is not coming–it's here. And those who yield to it will carry it to the ends of the earth.

Every historic move of the Spirit began with a single cry: "Lord, start with me." It didn't begin with strategy. It began with hunger. God doesn't look for the talented. He looks for the thirsty. The flames of revival and awakening are kindled in people who refuse to settle for a lukewarm Christian experience. God always responds to hunger. From Hannah's prayer in the temple to Elijah's altar on Mount Carmel, an outpouring of fire has always been born from desperate hearts. The difference between the ordinary believer and the revivalist is not talent–it's travail.

The cry of revival is the burdened heart that says, "I must

have more of You, Lord." God responds when a soul cries out like that. When you stop being satisfied with everything that is competing with the presence of God in your life, and you make room for His fire, God will send His fire.

The true evidence of revival is a burden for souls. When your heart burns for Jesus, it will burn for the lost. The same Spirit who fills you will compel you to reach lost souls.

> *"For the Son of Man has come to seek and to save that which was lost."–Luke 19:10*

And the moment your personal fire becomes missional, revival spreads. What God does in you, He intends to do through you. A heart that burns with love for Jesus will always become a light for the world. God can save a nation through one person fully yielded to Him. He's looking for modern-day Elijahs, Esthers, and Pauls–those who will say, "Here I am, Lord. Send me."

> *"For the eyes of the Lord run to and fro throughout the whole earth, to show Himself strong on behalf of those whose heart is loyal to Him."–2 Chronicles 16:9*

Revival fire falls on those who have made their hearts an altar and their lives a living sacrifice. If you keep your heart burning, you'll carry the fires of revival everywhere you go.

Revival doesn't start in a stadium–it starts in you.

THE PRESENCE THAT CHANGES EVERYTHING

You were created for the presence of God. From Eden to eternity, God's desire has been to dwell with His people. The fire that fell on the altar in the Old Testament, the glory that filled the tabernacle, and the wind that filled the upper room all point to one truth–God wants Heaven to invade Earth.

Revival is not man reaching up to God–it's God filling the space we've made for Him. He doesn't just want to visit us. He wants to inhabit. When the Church becomes a dwelling place instead of a place of entertainment and performance, revival fire will burn without ceasing.

The purpose of revival is to make Jesus real again in the hearts of His people. Everything changes when this becomes the highest priority. The early Church turned the world upside down because this truth was real to them. They preached Jesus. They carried God's presence and power and fire. And when we seek Him more than anything else, revival comes, and when God's presence takes over, the lost are saved, the saints are revived and miracles, signs and wonders break out.

When the presence of God fills a place, there's a weight that human words cannot describe. In the Bible, this is called the *kabod*–the tangible glory of God that rests upon His people.

> *"And it came to pass, when the priests came out of the holy place... that the house of the Lord was filled with a cloud, so that the priests could not continue ministering because of the cloud; for the glory of the Lord filled the house of God."* –2 Chronicles 5:13–14

When God's glory becomes real, human ability fades away. The weight of God's presence silences striving and exalts Him. When God's glory invades, all performance and entertainment, pride and religion just don't fit. They can't fit. That all has to be surrendered and consumed by the fire or it will repel God's glory and the atmosphere of Heaven will quickly pull away. Services that host revival fire may start with music and preaching, but they always end in awe.

The fire that once filled the temple now fills the believer. You are the ark of His presence–the dwelling place of His Spirit. Everywhere you go, you carry the same presence that raised Christ from the dead.

> *"But we all, with unveiled face, beholding as in a mirror the glory of the Lord, are being transformed into the same image from glory to glory, just as by the Spirit of the Lord."* –2 Corinthians 3:18

The presence that changes you will change the world through you.

Faith and hunger keep the flame alive. Revival fire is sustained through faithfulness.

"Be fervent in spirit, serving the Lord."–Romans 12:11

Fervency means "boiling over." That doesn't happen by accident. It's a continual choice to choose prayer over laziness, praise over complacency, and conviction over popularity. The fire doesn't die because the enemy attacks–it dies when the believer stops stirring it. You don't wait for revival to stir you. You stir revival within you. Every praise, every act of obedience, every sacrifice, every "yes" to God and every "no" to the enemy adds fuel to the fire.

REVIVAL FIRE AND THE POWER OF GOD

When revival fire comes, the natural becomes supernatural. Ordinary believers become miracle carriers. The gifts of the Spirit flow with ease. Lives are changed in moments that would take years without the anointing. The Church becomes what it was always meant to be–a house of miracles, healing, freedom, and transformation.

When revival fire burns, signs follow–not to glorify man, but to awaken nations to the reality of Jesus Christ.

When the Holy Spirit ignites your life, His flame becomes a global calling. The fire that begins in your heart will spread. God's plan has always been generational and it has always been global. From the outpouring at Pentecost to the awakening in our day, His purpose remains unchanged–to fill the whole earth with His presence. Revival is the heartbeat of Heaven for every tribe and tongue.

When the Holy Spirit fell on the early believers, He filled them and then sent them. The upper room became a launching pad for world evangelism. The fire that burned in Jerusalem spread to Antioch, Ephesus, Corinth, and beyond and that same fire burns in us.

> *"And you shall be witnesses to Me in Jerusalem, and in all Judea and Samaria, and to the end of the earth."–Acts 1:8*

Fire moves outward. That is simply the nature of fire. The evidence of the fire of God is the desire to go. Every encounter with God carries an assignment and those who have truly been set on fire will go wherever the Holy Spirit leads. Sometimes that's to a family member or a stranger or a neighbor, to tell them about Jesus, and sometimes it's to Asia or Africa.

When revival fire touches a believer, missions is no longer an option–it's their identity. God's mission to reach the lost to the ends of the earth, becomes theirs.

The Holy Spirit is orchestrating a global move of God in our lifetime. From underground churches in Asia to revival in Africa, Latin America, and beyond, the fire is spreading. It cannot be stopped by persecution or by politics. It cannot be stopped by any demonic agenda or by any antichrist spirit. A global outpouring is upon us.

> *"For the earth will be filled with the knowledge of the glory of the Lord as the waters cover the sea."–Habakkuk 2:14*

We are living in the days the prophets longed to see. Technology, travel, and global communication are tools we have to fulfill God's purposes at a more rapid rate. The gospel is reaching places once considered unreachable. Every service, every prayer gathering, every evangelistic crusade are parts of one great global harvest.

God is not preparing the Church to retreat. He's preparing her to invade and advance.

The fire of revival turns ordinary people into messengers of fire. Some will cross oceans; others will cross streets. Every believer is called to carry the flame of Christ's love to those still in darkness.

> *"How then shall they call on Him in whom they have not believed? And how shall they believe in Him of whom they have not heard? And how shall they hear without a preacher?"–Romans 10:14*

When revival fills a heart, burning ones live for one purpose–to make Jesus known. They carry the message of The Cross and the power of the resurrection. But the Spirit doesn't send us with words alone–He sends us with demonstration. The gospel must be preached with love and confirmed with power.

> *"Then He called His twelve disciples together and gave them power and authority over all demons, and to cure diseases. He sent them to preach the kingdom of God and to heal the sick."– Luke 9:1–2*

The world is waiting for a Church that not only preaches but demonstrates Jesus. The outpouring we're experiencing now is only the beginning. The Spirit is preparing a global Bride, purified by fire and filled with power. This final move of God will not be small or hidden–it will be worldwide. Entire nations will turn to Christ as the fire of revival spreads through yielded believers.

This is the hour to rise, to go, and to carry the fire of God fearlessly and unashamedly.

UNTIL THE WHOLE WORLD BURNS FOR JESUS

The end-time Church will not limp across the finish line. We will burn across it.

> *"And this gospel of the kingdom will be preached in all the world*

as a witness to all the nations, and then the end will come."–Matthew 24:14

We are the generation chosen to carry the flame to the ends of the earth. The Holy Spirit is calling His people: "Go in My power. Go with My fire." When the Church carries revival fire to the nations, the Great Commission becomes the Great Completion.

Heaven is not waiting for permission. The invasion has already begun. When Jesus stepped into the world, He didn't come as a negotiator. He came as a conqueror. Every miracle, every deliverance, and every soul set free was a strike against the dominion of darkness. When He said, *"Thy kingdom come, Thy will be done, on earth as it is in Heaven"* (Matthew 6:10), it wasn't a nice, little prayer to be religiously memorized and repeated. It was a declaration of war. Heaven was invading.

From that moment, hell has been on defense. Calvary was not a defeat. It was an ambush. The Cross was the weapon that shattered the enemy's command post. The empty tomb was Heaven's victory shout echoing through every generation. Now, the same Spirit that raised Christ from the dead is igniting His Church with fire once again. This is Heaven's counterstrike.

We are not spectators of revival–we are its carriers. The fire of the Holy Spirit is the artillery of Heaven. It invades atmospheres and breaks through every demonic power that thought it owned the ground. Revival occupies and the

Kingdom of Heaven is taking territory–through your voice, through your life, and through your fire.

When the Kingdom of God invades, nothing stays the same. Blind eyes open. Deaf ears unstop. Tumors disappear. Captives are freed. Addicts are delivered. Families are restored. Cities are saved. And this time, He is doing it through you.

You are Heaven's invasion point. You are not here to survive the last days–you are here to enforce Heaven's rule upon the earth. Every prayer you pray, every truth you speak, every soul you win–it's another banner raised in enemy territory. Revival fire is not coming someday. It's here, burning now, sweeping through those who dare to say, "Lord, use me."

The Day is approaching (Hebrews 10:25), the coming of the Lord is at hand (James 5:8). The skies are opening. The armies of Heaven are advancing. The fire of God is falling to invade the darkness. Heaven's invasion has begun. A global outpouring of God's fire has been unleashed. Make room for God and let revival fire spread through you.

FIVE
HISTORY OF REVIVAL FIRE

"I know not what course others may take; but as for me, give me revival in my soul and in my church and in my nation–or give me death!" –Leonard Ravenhill

THE EARLY CHURCH–THE FIRST OUTPOURING

Every great revival in history traces back to one moment–the day of Pentecost.

This was the first time the fire of God was poured out not on an altar of stone, but on hearts of flesh. It marked the beginning of the Church's power and mission.

"When the Day of Pentecost had fully come, they were all with one accord in one place. And suddenly there came a sound from

Heaven, as of a rushing mighty wind, and it filled the whole house where they were sitting. Then there appeared to them divided tongues, as of fire, and one sat upon each of them. And they were all filled with the Holy Spirit."–Acts 2:1–4

That moment changed everything. Revival was no longer something to wait for. It had arrived.

THE BIRTH OF THE CHURCH IN FIRE

The Church was born in a sudden moment of wind and fire and it grew through bold witnesses who refused to cower to persecution, threats of death, or any opposition. Before Pentecost, the disciples had theology but after Pentecost, they had power. Jesus had told them to wait until they were endued with power from on high (Luke 24:49), and when the fire came, it transformed them completely. The Church's first breath was revival.

The fire of God became the Church's identity. They didn't need status. They didn't have buildings. They didn't have programs–they had power.

The early believers were carriers of the fire of God and within decades, the gospel spread across continents, not through technology or wealth, but through Spirit-filled men and women burning with conviction.

"And daily in the temple, and in every house, they did not cease teaching and preaching Jesus as the Christ."–Acts 5:42

This was revival. Miracles confirmed their message. Communities were transformed. Cities like Antioch, Ephesus, and Corinth became hubs of the supernatural. The fire that fell burned in homes, markets, and prisons and the Church grew not by strategy, but because of fire. The early Church was unstoppable because it was uncontainable. Persecution scattered believers–but everywhere they went, revival spread.

Pentecost wasn't a one-time event–it was the prototype for every future awakening. Every revival since has been a rediscovery of what was poured out that day: the presence, power, fire and purpose of the Holy Spirit.

"Repent, and let every one of you be baptized in the name of Jesus Christ for the remission of sins; and you shall receive the gift of the Holy Spirit."–Acts 2:38

The history of revival begins, and continues, with Pentecost.

THE GREAT AWAKENINGS–FIRE IN THE NATIONS

After the fire of Pentecost, revival continued to spread for centuries.

From the Roman Empire to remote villages, the gospel burned across the world, but by the 17th and 18th centuries, much of the Church had grown cold. Then, God struck the match again.

Through the Great Awakenings, entire nations were set on fire with the presence of God. When humanity forgot God, His Spirit reminded them. When Christianity became ritual, He made it real again. Revival fire began to sweep through nations once more, proving that God's power still meets hungry people.

THE FIRST GREAT AWAKENING (1730S–1750S)

The First Great Awakening began in the early 1700s, mainly in Britain and the American colonies.

At that time, churches were formal, sermons were intellectual, and people attended services without transformation. Then, God raised up men who carried the flame–John Wesley, George Whitefield, and Jonathan Edwards.

Their preaching was not polished but powerful. They declared repentance, holiness, and the new birth through the Holy Spirit. Crowds wept and trembled. Multitudes cried out for salvation. Entire towns changed. Taverns closed. Crime rates dropped. The spiritual atmosphere of nations shifted.

The First Great Awakening proved that true revival reforms hearts and societies. It turned dry religion into living devotion and laid the foundation for evangelistic missions around the world.

THE SECOND GREAT AWAKENING (1790S–1840S)

By the late 1700s, another wave of revival swept through America and Europe.

Churches were declining, immorality was rising, and atheism was spreading. But once again, God found hungry hearts–this time in prayer meetings and outdoor gatherings.

Leaders like Charles Finney, Peter Cartwright, and Francis Asbury became flames in the hand of God. Camp meetings drew thousands. Finney's revival services emphasized conviction, confession, and conversion. People wept for their sin and left transformed.

The Second Great Awakening didn't just fill altars. It filled the world with missions. Bible societies, abolition movements, and evangelistic organizations were born from its fire. It revived individuals, but it also awakened an entire generation's sense of purpose in God.

LATER AWAKENINGS (1850S–1900S)

God continued to move in waves.

In 1857, Jeremiah Lanphier, a businessman in New York, started a noon prayer meeting that grew from six men to thousands across the city. Soon, revival swept the nation, touching over one million people. Historians called it The Prayer Revival of 1857–1858.

At the same time, revival fires burned in Wales, Ireland, and Scotland. Churches overflowed. Newspapers reported conversions. The presence of God was tangible in entire cities.

Then, toward the end of the 19th century, the holiness and healing movements began preparing the way for what would soon erupt in Los Angeles–the greatest outpouring since Pentecost itself.

The Great Awakenings were not just moments in history. Every outpouring reminded the Church that God still answers the cries of His people with fire.

AZUSA STREET–THE BIRTH OF MODERN PENTECOST

By the early 1900s, the Church had grown respectable but powerless.

Many believed the miracles of Scripture had ended, and

the baptism of the Holy Spirit was only a doctrine, not an experience.

But God was about to remind the world that His fire never dies.

> "For I will pour water on him who is thirsty, and floods on the dry ground; I will pour My Spirit on your descendants, and My blessing on your offspring."–Isaiah 44:3

In a small mission building on Azusa Street in Los Angeles, revival broke out that would shake the world. It wasn't led by famous preachers, but by humble, hungry hearts.

THE MAN GOD USED: WILLIAM J. SEYMOUR

The vessel God chose to make a flame was William J. Seymour, the son of former slaves from Louisiana. He was blind in one eye and poor by the world's standards. But he was rich in faith. Seymour had been deeply influenced by the holiness movement and the teachings on the baptism of the Holy Spirit. He believed that God still poured out the same fire that fell in the book of Acts and he was determined to seek it.

After arriving in Los Angeles in 1906, Seymour began preaching in a small home on Bonnie Brae Street. People gathered to pray earnestly for the Holy Spirit. Then, suddenly the fire fell. Men and women began speaking in tongues, weeping, and trembling under the power of God.

The gatherings grew so large that the porch collapsed from the crowds, forcing them to move to a vacant building at 312 Azusa Street–a place that would soon become known around the world.

THE OUTPOURING ON AZUSA STREET

The meetings at Azusa were unlike anything most had ever seen.

There were no programs, no famous choirs, no schedules; only prayer, worship, and the tangible presence of God. The services ran day and night. People would come in and immediately feel conviction, fall to their knees, and cry out to God for mercy. Others received healing, deliverance, and the baptism of the Holy Spirit with the evidence of speaking in tongues.

The atmosphere was electric but it was reverent. Seymour would usually kneel behind the pulpit with his head inside a wooden crate, praying quietly while others ministered. There was no personality or performance–only the presence of God.

History reports that on more than one occasion, bystanders called the fire department to report a visible fire blazing on the roof of 312 Azusa Street. But the fire was supernatural and when firefighters arrived, they found no natural fire, just the sound of worship from within the building and flames dancing on the roof top as Heaven invaded Earth.

Visitors from across the nation and around the world came to witness the move. Journalists mocked it, but Heaven blessed it.

THE SPIRIT OF UNITY AND POWER

What made Azusa truly revolutionary was not only its power but its unity. In a deeply segregated America, people of every race, age, and background worshiped side by side, experiencing the Holy Spirit together.

This broke cultural barriers and released a prophetic picture of the Kingdom of God on earth. The revival didn't just heal bodies–it healed divisions. The presence of God tore down walls that religion and society had built.

This is still the answer that our dark world needs: a fire that burns until the darkness breaks.

THE GLOBAL IMPACT

From that small mission on Azusa Street, missionaries and preachers went forth carrying the flame of Pentecost to every continent. Within months, reports of similar outpourings came from India, Korea, Africa, and Latin America.

The modern Pentecostal movement was born, eventually

giving rise to multiple denominations as well as later charismatic and independent Spirit-filled movements.

> *"And the Lord added to the church daily those who were being saved."*–Acts 2:47

What began as a humble prayer meeting became a global fire that continues to burn today. Over a century later, hundreds of millions of Spirit-filled believers trace their spiritual heritage back to that tiny room on Azusa Street.

THE LESSON AND WARNING OF AZUSA

The Azusa revival teaches us that God looks for those who thirst for Him.

The legacy of Azusa Street is so clear: The Spirit falls where people are hungry for Him more than anything else and that same life-changing, all-consuming revival fire that fell on Azusa Street is available today for anyone who will kneel, pray, and believe.

We must see that we have downgraded the Holy Spirit to one baptism when there are many subsequent overflowings.

We are a Spirit-filled movement. We must go back and seek a fresh fire. Before we petition a congressman, protest in front of a clinic, yell at demons, or anything else, we must have a new Day of Pentecost. We must form upper rooms in every Spirit-filled ministry.

This is a warning to everyone who speaks in tongues. We must repent and be refilled in the Holy Spirit and fire so that we have real power and authority to do the true work of God.

God looks for those who thirst for Him.

REVIVALISTS WHO CARRIED THE FLAME– FINNEY, WESLEY, WIGGLESWORTH, AND OTHERS

Throughout history, God has always had a remnant; people who refused to live without His presence.

When the Church grew cold, He raised up men and women who burned. These were individuals so surrendered that their lives became living sermons of the Spirit's power. These revivalists were flames of God's presence. They believed God's Word, obeyed His voice, and paid any price to see souls saved and nations awakened.

Their stories remind us that revival is not an event–it's a person fully yielded to God. Each carried a unique flame of Heaven's fire, but all burned with the same Holy Ghost power.

JOHN WESLEY–FIRE OF HOLINESS

In the 1700s, John Wesley became one of the greatest revival leaders in history.

A scholar at Oxford and an Anglican minister, he had all

the form of religion but none of its fire–until his heart was "strangely warmed" at a Moravian meeting in London in 1738. That moment changed everything.

> *"I felt my heart strangely warmed. I felt I did trust in Christ, Christ alone for salvation."*–John Wesley

Empowered by the Spirit, Wesley traveled over 250,000 miles on horseback, preaching thousands of sermons across England and America.

He emphasized holiness, repentance, and sanctification through the power of the Holy Spirit. Under his ministry, countless lives were transformed, and the Methodist movement was born.

Wesley's fire was not emotionalism–it was disciplined devotion. He believed that holiness and the Holy Spirit's power were inseparable. His revival turned a morally declining England back to God.

CHARLES FINNEY–FIRE OF CONVICTION

In the 1800s, Charles G. Finney emerged as the voice of the Second Great Awakening.

A lawyer turned preacher, Finney carried a fiery boldness that shook cities.

His sermons pierced hearts with conviction so deeply

that entire communities would weep in repentance before he even began to preach.

> *"Revival comes from Heaven when heroic souls enter the conflict determined to win or die—or if need be, to win and die."—Charles Finney*

Finney's ministry was marked by deep conviction and moral reform. He believed revival was not a mystery but a result of obedience—that if people prayed, repented, and sought God wholeheartedly, revival would come.

Under his preaching, bars closed, crime dropped, and thousands were converted. He trained young ministers in revival principles, establishing schools that produced generations of evangelists.

Finney's legacy was one of truth with power and conviction that led to transformation.

SMITH WIGGLESWORTH—FIRE OF POWER

In the early 1900s, Smith Wigglesworth, a plumber from England, became one of the most remarkable evangelists of his time.

Uneducated but full of the Holy Spirit, he operated in a level of faith and power rarely seen since the apostles.

"I'm not moved by what I see or feel, but only by what I believe. And I believe the Word of God."–Smith Wigglesworth

Wigglesworth saw the dead raised, the sick healed, and thousands filled with the Holy Spirit. He preached repentance, holiness, and the fullness of the Holy Spirit with boldness.

His ministry wasn't built on eloquence, but on obedience. He once said, "If the Spirit doesn't move me, I move the Spirit." He lived a life of total dependence on God's power. Everywhere he went, revival fire followed.

EVAN ROBERTS–FIRE OF INTERCESSION

In 1904, in Wales, Evan Roberts became the spark for one of the most powerful revivals in modern history.

At only 26 years old, he carried a deep burden for souls and prayed for revival with tears and travail.

"Bend the Church, and save the world."–Evan Roberts

His meetings were simple–prayer, confession, worship, and obedience to the Holy Spirit. But under his leadership, over 100,000 people were saved in just a few months.

Churches overflowed, bars closed, and even the police had nothing to do because crime vanished. The Welsh

Revival influenced movements across the world, including the Azusa Street outpouring two years later.

Roberts taught the power of personal purity, humility, and prayer–that revival begins when the Church is "bent" in surrender before God.

MARIA WOODWORTH-ETTER–FIRE OF THE SPIRIT

Maria Woodworth-Etter was a pioneer of Pentecostal power before Azusa ever began.

In the late 1800s, this bold woman of God preached to multitudes across America with extraordinary miracles and signs following.

> *"When the power of God comes down, sinners shake and quake. The devil knows he has to go."–Maria Woodworth-Etter*

Crowds gathered as people fell under conviction, cried out for salvation, and were miraculously healed. She endured mockery and opposition but pressed on with courage.

Her ministry blazed a trail for Spirit-filled women in ministry and inspired later revivalists like Aimee Semple McPherson and Kathryn Kuhlman.

AIMEE SEMPLE MCPHERSON–FIRE OF CREATIVITY AND EVANGELISM

In the early 20th century, Aimee Semple McPherson became one of the most influential evangelists in America.

Known for her dramatic preaching style, healing crusades, and creative use of media, she brought revival to cities and helped start the Foursquare Church.

> *"We are not to be weak, wobbly Christians, but strong soldiers of The Cross."*–Aimee Semple McPherson

Her ministry combined holiness and joy, conviction and compassion, and faith and creativity. She used radio broadcasts and stage presentations to share the gospel with millions. McPherson proved that revival could be both spiritual and strategic, reaching the lost in every possible way.

CATHERINE BOOTH AND WILLIAM BOOTH–FIRE OF COMPASSION

Founders of The Salvation Army, William and Catherine Booth brought revival to the streets of London. They believed the gospel was not just for the church pew but for the poorest, most broken people of society.

"You cannot warm the hearts of people with God's love if they have an empty stomach and cold feet."–William Booth

Their movement combined evangelism with social compassion, rescuing prostitutes, feeding the hungry, and preaching salvation to the forgotten.

Their fire of compassion proved that revival is not only about power–it's also about love in action.

THEIR LEGACY: LIVING FLAMES

These revivalists remind us that God uses ordinary people to do extraordinary things. Each one had a different gift, a different calling, and lived at a different time–but they all had the same Holy Spirit.

Their lives still preach: Holiness matters. Prayer works. The Holy Ghost still moves in power. One person on fire can change the world.

If history teaches us anything, it is that God doesn't change His methods–only His messengers. Revival is not locked in the past; it is waiting in the hearts of those willing to follow the same path. What God did through Wesley, Finney, Roberts, and Seymour, He can do again through anyone willing to pay the price.

WHAT THESE REVIVALS TEACH US TODAY

The study of revival is not a trip through history–it is an invitation. Every story of fire that fell before us was meant to awaken a cry within us. God uses the history of revival to instruct us. God's methods are the same. His desire for His Church has not shifted. His power has not weakened. The only question that remains is whether His people will once again make room for Him to move and be filled with Him to burn.

Every revival in history began in dark times. The Church was cold, society was wicked, and sin was celebrated. But it was in those very moments that the light of God broke through the strongest. Revival is not hindered by darkness–it shines brightest in it.

> *"The light shines in the darkness, and the darkness did not comprehend it."–John 1:5*

If God could shake nations when communication was slow and travel was dangerous, how much more could He move today? The problem has never been with God. It has been with us.

These outpourings began with one or two people who refused to live without God's presence. A lonely preacher in England. A young woman in prayer. A small group of believers in a home. You do not have to be known by the world to be used by Heaven. Revival begins the moment you say, "Lord, whatever it takes–start in me."

These men and women, although revivalists, were ordinary by human standards. Most were untrained, unqualified, and underestimated. But they yielded completely, and God used them mightily.

The pattern remains. God uses the foolish things of the world to display His glory.

> *"But God has chosen the foolish things of the world to put to shame the wise, and God has chosen the weak things of the world to put to shame the things which are mighty."–1 Corinthians 1:27*

You might not have status or influence, but you can have surrender and sacrifice. You can pray and fast. You can pursue and make room for God to pour out His Spirit and fire in your life. If you do your part, God will send His fire.

THE CALL TO THIS GENERATION

We stand now at the threshold of another great move of God. Our world mirrors the conditions of every age before great outpourings of God–darkness increasing, sin celebrated, and truth mocked. But this is the soil where revival thrives.

If we will advance, if we will burn, and if we refuse to quit, we will see what the prophets longed to see–a global awakening before the return of Christ. The Spirit of God is stirring His Church again. The fire is not coming–it is already here.

This is our moment to carry the flame forward. The torch that passed from Pentecost to Wesley, from Finney to Seymour, is now being handed to us. We are not called to admire their stories but to continue them. An upper room wind is blowing now.

The Holy Ghost who made the saints of history, flames, is ready to fill you. History was not meant to end with their revival–it was meant to ignite ours.

The chronicles of revival are records of war–outpourings of light in the midst of darkness; compelling men and women to rise up, in the power of God, and advance. Every generation that burned with Heaven's fire stood on battlefields soaked in prayer and marked by blood. These revivalists were men and women possessed by the Holy Ghost and carrying the torch of holy invasion into territories ruled by darkness. They did not blend in. They burned through.

From generation to generation, the torch has passed through the hands of those who dared to believe that one life set on fire could shake a nation. They were mocked, threatened, imprisoned, and misunderstood–but they could not be silenced and they would not quit. Their fire burned too deep.

When Gideon hid in the winepress, fearful and defeated, God called him by a name he didn't feel worthy of–*"Mighty man of valor."* (Judges 6:12). Israel was enslaved, their altars torn down, their courage stripped away. But when the Spirit of the Lord came upon Gideon, a trembling farmer became a warrior. Three hundred men, armed with torches and trumpets, not swords, destroyed the armies of Midian. The strategy made no sense but Heaven's power doesn't depend on human logic. When the jars broke and the fire blazed into the night, confusion fell on the enemy's camp and the darkness scattered before the light.

That is what revival looks like. A remnant, weak in the world's eyes, carrying a flame into impossible odds and burning until the fire breaks through the darkness. Just like God called Gideon from hiding, He is calling His Church from the shadows. The fire that burned in their torches now burns in ours.

The history of revival is the history of ordinary men and women who became extraordinary when the fire of God ignited them. They were not professionals. They were possessed. They were soldiers, unafraid to stand in the ashes of compromise and cry out for the wind of God to blow again; they were the living sacrifice on the altar that God could ignite. And they were unafraid to look the devil eye to eye and advance into enemy territory for the glory of God and the cause of Christ.

Throughout the centuries, Heaven's flame has found new warriors. When the darkness smothered the Church, Martin Luther lit the torch of truth and nailed it to the gates of religion. When complacency paralyzed the faith, John Knox declared, "Give me Scotland or I die!" and God gave him a nation. When the world mocked holiness, John Wesley caught fire, and Britain ran to watch him burn. When despair covered Wales, Evan Roberts wept until Heaven heard and answered. When spiritual death suffocated England, Smith Wigglesworth rose up with miracle fire in his veins and shouted, "Faith is the flame that reaches the heart of God!" Charles Finney walked into cities and watched entire communities bow before God. William Booth marched into the gutters of London, declaring, "While there remains one dark soul without the light of God, I'll fight!"

They were not great because of talent–they were great because they burned. The world tried to extinguish their flame, but every attempt only made it brighter. They stood between Heaven and hell, torchbearers of holy fire, advancing the kingdom one soul at a time. Every one of them stood where you now stand. Every one of them faced the same darkness that faces this hour. They did not have better times–they simply had what the hour called for–a burning Spirit. They were the flames that refused to go out in the darkness.

And now, the torch has been pressed into your hands. The battle is not coming–it's here. Heaven's invasion has already begun, and you are part of the front line. The call of God in this hour is not to study the fire but to carry it. We don't need historians of revival right now; that is not what this hour is calling for–we need soldiers of fire. The same Spirit that raised Jesus from the dead is searching for those who will not shrink back when the battle rages but will stand as living walls of fire until the darkness collapses and the Kingdom of God advances.

This is the hour for holy aggression. Hell has waged open war against the purposes of God and Heaven is answering with fire. The warriors of old are watching from the stands of eternity. Their race is finished but ours is not. The sound of marching fills the Heavens, and the shout of the King is in our camp.

This is an invasion. The torch has been passed. You have been entrusted with a sacred flame–don't drop it, don't hide it, and don't let that fire grow dim. Fan it until it consumes everything within you that resists the call of God. Run your race as a torchbearer of revival fire. Let your prayers be like trumpets in the night and let your life burn until hell trembles at the sound of your footsteps.

The warriors before you carried the fire through the ages. Now it burns in your hands. This is your moment. This is your war.

SIX
PRAYER THAT SHAKES HEAVEN AND DISMANTLES HELL

"Prayer breaks all bars, dissolves all chains, opens all prisons, and widens all straits by which God's saints have been held."
–E.M. Bounds

Hell is advancing without apology, and the Church can no longer afford to whisper while the kingdom of darkness screams. This is war and our greatest weapon is prayer.

Prayer is not always a calm conversation with God. It is also a violent confrontation between two Kingdoms. It is where a vessel becomes the bridge between Heaven's plan and Earth's reality. It is where the voice of man becomes the hammer of Heaven. True prayer tears through layers of resistance and calls the power of God down upon the battlefield of life.

When a believer begins to pray in the Spirit, the unseen realm begins to shake. Angels move. Strongholds weaken. Demons scatter. The tide of the battle shifts. Prayer is not what you do after you fight. It is the fight. The war begins and is won when knees hit the ground.

Look at the Early Church in the book of Acts. Threatened by rulers and silenced by fear, they didn't retreat. They prayed. And the place where they were gathered was shaken. They walked out of that prayer meeting as men and women the world and the devil could no longer defeat.

Think of Daniel in Babylon. The empire around him bowed to idols, but he knelt three times a day and prayed until the Heavens opened. For twenty-one days the prince of Persia resisted the answer, but Daniel didn't quit. His intercession reached beyond kings and tore through principalities. Prayer is not hindered by delay. It digs in deeper until the walls of hell collapse.

And in that prison cell at midnight, Paul and Silas prayed until the ground shook. Their chains fell, the doors swung open, and the darkness was shattered by the sound of their praise. That's what happens when prayer carries fire–it breaks what was unbreakable. It sets captives free who didn't even know deliverance was possible.

This is the missing weapon of our generation. We've learned how to organize but forgotten how to agonize. We've built stages but we've neglected altars. We've gathered crowds but lack power. Prayer is what turns gatherings into battlegrounds. It's what turns weak men into warriors. Without prayer, there is no authority.

The prayers that shake Heaven are not quiet or polite. They are desperate. They rise from hearts that refuse to let hell win. They are soaked in tears and born from burden. They don't read from a script. They cry from the depths of travail. The saints who move the world are those who kneel in prayer first.

This is your battleground. The enemy has drawn his lines, but Heaven is looking for soldiers who will fight on their knees. The Spirit is calling for intercessors; those who will not sleep through the shaking, who will not watch from the sidelines, but who will step into the fire of prayer until Heaven invades the earth.

Stop praying small prayers. Pray with power that breaks the atmosphere. Pray like a warrior whose words are weapons. Pray until chains rattle and demons flee. The weapon is in your mouth and the battlefield is right in front of you. Pray until the Heavens shake and the darkness around you dismantles. Pray until the glory of God floods the earth.

THE POWER OF PRAYER IN REVIVAL

Prayer is the furnace of revival.

Every outpouring of God's Spirit has been preceded by people who refused to stop praying until Heaven answered.

Revival is not produced by preaching, programs, or strategy. It is birthed in prayer. When God finds a praying people, He raises up a burning Church.

> *"If My people who are called by My name will humble themselves, and pray and seek My face, and turn from their wicked ways, then I will hear from Heaven, and will forgive their sin and heal their land."*–2 Chronicles 7:14

That one verse summarizes the formula for revival. God responds to humility, hunger, and prayer.

Prayer is the bridge between earth's need and Heaven's supply. It invites divine power into human weakness. Every time God's people prayed earnestly, Heaven invaded. Wherever prayer rises, power will fall.

No revival can survive without it. Preaching can draw attention, but prayer draws God. When the Church stops praying, the fire fades. But when prayer is restored, the flame returns stronger than before.

Revival is not about convincing God to move–it's about aligning ourselves with Him. Prayer doesn't change God; it changes us. It burns away pride, impatience, and unbelief until we can carry what He wants to give.

> *"Your kingdom come. Your will be done on earth as it is in Heaven."*–Matthew 6:10

That prayer was not meant to be a ritual–it was meant to be a reality. When we pray, "Your will be done," we're inviting Heaven's plans to overtake ours; Heaven's will being done on earth through yielded people.

The spiritual temperature of a church or a nation can be measured by its prayer life. When prayer weakens, faith weakens. When prayer strengthens, fire strengthens.

"Ask, and it will be given to you; seek, and you will find; knock, and it will be opened to you."–Matthew 7:7

Asking opens doors. Seeking discovers God's heart. Knocking breaks through resistance. Prayer is the invitation that God never ignores. This secret to revival hasn't changed–those who kneel in prayer will stand in power.

Prayer is the moment Heaven touches earth through surrendered hearts. Prayer is literally the bridge between Heaven and Earth, the connection point between two realms and the door that opens the flow of Heaven into Earth. The greatest moves of God in history were started by men and women who learned to pray when no one was watching. Their reward was not attention. Their reward was visitation.

"The Lord is near to all who call upon Him, to all who call upon Him in truth."–Psalm 145:18

The same is true today.

THE PRAYER THAT MOVES GOD

Not all prayer moves God.

There are prayers that are routine, and there are prayers that reach the throne. The difference is not eloquence or knowledge but desire and desperation. God responds to burning hearts not perfect wording.

The prayer that moves God is the prayer that costs something–time, pride, convenience, comfort. It is the cry of desperation–the kind that refuses to be denied. And it attracts the presence of God.

> *"As the deer pants for the water brooks, so pants my soul for You, O God."–Psalm 42:1*

This kind of prayer does not politely request; it pleads. It doesn't schedule God for a moment. It waits on Him until He comes. Desperate prayer is what separates God seekers from average church attenders.

God is uniquely drawn to the sound of holy hunger. Heaven always answers.

Faith is a necessary weapon in prayer. Desperation without faith produces frustration, but faith gives prayer power. Faith is not positive thinking. It is unwavering trust in a faithful God. When you pray believing that God will move, your words become weapons.

"And whatever things you ask in prayer, believing, you will receive."–Matthew 21:22

Faith turns petitions into declarations. It stands on the Word, even when nothing seems to change. It believes that what God has promised, He will perform.

In revival atmospheres, the Church stops praying "if" prayers and starts praying "when" prayers–believers move from doubt to expectation.

The prayer that moves God is bold. It dares to ask for rain in a drought. It speaks to mountains that others have learned to walk around. God is moved by faith that refuses to quit.

Another important weapon is the weapon of obedience in prayer. The prayer that moves God must also move us. Prayer is not complete when we speak–it is complete when we obey. Revival fire does not come through prayer alone, but through prayer that produces action. God usually responds to obedience faster than words.

When the Spirit prompts you to forgive, to give, to go, to humble yourself, to share the gospel with someone, to cast out a devil, or to pray for someone–obedience becomes the door through which power flows. The revival you're praying for might be waiting on the obedience you're avoiding.

The weapon of persistence in prayer is most commonly left out. Some prayers are answered instantly but others are answered through endurance.

And revival praying requires persistence. The greatest

intercessors in history were those who refused to stop praying, even when nothing seemed to happen.

> *"Then He spoke a parable to them, that men always ought to pray and not lose heart."–Luke 18:1*

Persistence proves faith. It shows God that you desire Him more than convenience. It shows God that you believe Him at His Word even when you don't see it in the natural. Breakthrough begins with someone who prays *one more time.*

When Elijah prayed for rain, nothing happened the first six times. But on the seventh, the cloud appeared. Persistence turns petitions into power.

If we persist in prayer and in faith and in obedience, we will see what others only dreamed of.

When desperation meets faith and when persistence meets humility– Heaven responds and fire falls. This is when dry altars ignite and the Church becomes the furnace of God's glory again.

> *"Then the fire of the Lord fell and consumed the burnt sacrifice."–1 Kings 18:38*

The prayer that moves God is the one that refuses to settle for anything less than His presence. True intercession is not praying for personal needs; it is standing in the gap for others until God's will is done on earth. Intercession is not casual prayer. It is costly prayer. It demands compassion, persistence, and spiritual authority. Intercession is how God uses His people to dismantle hell and shake Heaven until it invades earth.

> *"So I sought for a man among them who would make a wall, and stand in the gap before Me on behalf of the land, that I should not destroy it; but I found no one."–Ezekiel 22:30*

That verse shows God's heart and our responsibility. The Lord is looking for intercessors to agree with Him. He chooses to work through human vessels so that His glory might flow through surrendered lives.

God's plan involves partnership. He moves through people who pray.

Moses interceded for Israel, and judgment was withheld. Elijah prayed, and rain returned. Daniel prayed, and empires shifted.

Intercession connects Heaven's will with earthly obedience.

Intercessors carry what Scripture calls the burden of the Lord. It is a spiritual weight placed on the heart by the Holy Spirit. It is a deep, inescapable concern for souls, for the broken, and for God's will.

This burden cannot be created. It is caught in prayer. When you feel that heaviness in prayer; when tears come without explanation or when your spirit groans, you are experiencing intercession.

The Holy Spirit shares His heart with yours, and in that partnership, you begin to pray for what He desires most. Every great move of God has been birthed through burdens. Heaven answers the prayers that come from a heart burdened by God Himself.

STANDING IN THE GAP

To "stand in the gap" means to take spiritual responsibility where others have fallen short. An intercessor stands between judgment and mercy, pleading for God's will to triumph. The posture of an intercessor is both low and bold–low before God and bold before darkness. It is humility that recognizes dependence on God, and authority that declares His Word with confidence.

> *"Let us therefore come boldly to the throne of grace, that we may obtain mercy and find grace to help in time of need."–Hebrews 4:16*

This posture requires humility and courage. It means identifying with the sins of others, not as an accuser but as a mediator.

> "Then he said, 'O my God, I am too ashamed and humiliated to lift up my face to You, my God, for our iniquities have risen higher than our heads.'"–Ezra 9:6

Ezra, Nehemiah, and Daniel all prayed that way. They confessed their nation's sins as if they were their own.

True intercession does not pray from a distance–it steps into the need and carries it before God with compassion. Intercessors must carry both reverence and resolve. They bow before the King but command in His name. They are humble in spirit but fierce in faith.

In prayer, the intercessor kneels before Heaven and stands against hell. That is the heart of revival prayer–submission and authority working together to bring Heaven's will to earth. When believers embrace this posture–humble, faithful, and burdened, God hears and moves.

God uses intercession to change circumstances and release His power. When you pray for others, you align yourself with the heart of Jesus–the ultimate Intercessor who forever lives to make intercession for us.

> "Therefore He is also able to save to the uttermost those who come to God through Him, since He always lives to make intercession for them."–Hebrews 7:25

Intercession is the heartbeat of Christ expressed through His people.

It is not optional for revival–it is essential.

THE FIRE OF FERVENT PRAYER

There is another weapon of prayer that Heaven cannot ignore. It is not cold or calm. It is the kind that burns.

The early Church called it fervent prayer–prayer that comes from the heart, consumes the soul, and releases the fire of God on the earth.

> *"The effective, fervent prayer of a righteous man avails much."–James 5:16*

Fervent prayer is not louder; it's deeper. It doesn't always shout, but it always burns. It is the prayer of conviction, desperation, and an utter dependance on God. Wherever this kind of prayer is prayed, revival fire follows.

Fervent prayer is not mechanical or religious. It is alive with faith. It has been submerged in the oil of anointing. It bursts out like a river of living water from within a consecrated, burning vessel. It believes that what God has spoken, He will perform. When the heart believes, the words ignite.

> *"Whatever things you ask when you pray, believe that you receive them, and you will have them."–Mark 11:24*

Fervent prayer is the language of expectation. It prays as

though the answer has already begun to arrive. True fervency doesn't come from human emotion–it comes from a living relationship with Jesus. The closer you walk with Him, the more you feel what He feels and are burdened for what burdens Him. His desires become your desires. His burdens become your burdens.

One of the greatest enemies of fervent prayer is distraction. The enemy always wants to distract you from praying–and tries to keep you unfocused while you do.

Fervency means turning off the noise and fixing your attention on God until His presence becomes real.

> *"But you, when you pray, go into your room, and when you have shut your door, pray to your Father who is in the secret place."–Matthew 6:6*

To pray fervently, you have to pray intentionally. You can't stay on fire while scrolling through the world's noise. When you shut the door to distraction, you open the door to hear God.

Many scriptural breakthroughs were preceded by fervent prayer.

Hannah wept in prayer, and God gave her a son who became a prophet. Jesus prayed with such intensity in Gethsemane that His sweat became like great drops of blood. Elijah's prayer wasn't polished–it was powerful. He prayed until he saw the cloud. He prayed until Heaven responded.

> *"Then Elijah said to Ahab, 'Go up, eat and drink; for there is the sound of abundance of rain.' ... And Elijah went up to the top of Carmel; then he bowed down on the ground, and put his face between his knees."–1 Kings 18:41–42*

That is fervency. It refuses to quit until the answer arrives. Fervent prayer is not measured by emotion but by endurance. It stays on its knees until what was promised becomes visible.

You cannot sustain fervent prayer through willpower. Human strength runs out. The fire of revival prayer is supernatural. It is the work of the Holy Spirit within you.

Your part is to yield. His part is to supply the flame.

> *"Rejoicing in hope, patient in tribulation, continuing steadfastly in prayer."–Romans 12:12*

When the flesh grows weary, the Holy Spirit gives you strength. When the mind loses focus, the Holy Spirit intercedes with groanings too deep for words. The fire that begins in the Spirit must be maintained by the Spirit.

Fervent prayer is the sound of the Church crying, "Come, Lord Jesus." When believers begin to pray this way again–with faith, obedience, persistence, and fervency–revival fire falls in an ever increasing measure.

Fervent prayer is revival's oxygen.

THE ROLE OF THE HOLY SPIRIT IN PRAYER

The Holy Spirit is the heartbeat of all true prayer.

Without Him, prayer is just words. He is the One who teaches us what to pray, how to pray, and even gives us the strength to continue when we have none left. Every move of God that ever changed the world began when people prayed *in* the Spirit, not just *to* God.

> *"Likewise the Spirit also helps in our weaknesses. For we do not know what we should pray for as we ought, but the Spirit Himself makes intercession for us with groanings which cannot be uttered."*–Romans 8:26

When the Holy Spirit leads the prayer, the results always match Heaven's will. Many times, we don't have words to pray. There are moments when the need is too great, the pain is too deep, or the burden is too heavy to express. That is where the Holy Spirit steps in.

> *"For He who searches the hearts knows what the mind of the Spirit is, because He makes intercession for the saints according to the will of God."*–Romans 8:27

When you yield to Him in prayer, whether through groaning, weeping, or praying in tongues, the Spirit prays through you perfectly.

Your words may fail, but His never do. He knows exactly what needs to be said, because He knows the mind of God. That is why Holy Spirit-led prayer brings results that human strength cannot. It bypasses our limitations and connects directly to the throne of God.

The closer you walk with the Spirit, the more your desires align with God's desires. He reshapes your priorities until what matters to God matters to you. When you pray in the Spirit, your heart stops striving to change God's mind and starts agreeing with Him. You begin to pray with confidence, because you know your words are in alignment with His Word.

The Holy Spirit doesn't just help you pray–He prays through you. He uses your voice as a vessel for intercession. When you yield fully, the Spirit prays through you for things you could never comprehend–revival in nations, breakthroughs in families, healing for the sick, and salvation for souls you've never met.

> *"But you, beloved, building yourselves up on your most holy faith, praying in the Holy Spirit."–Jude 20*

Spirit-led prayer not only brings results–it strengthens you. Every time you pray in the Spirit, your faith grows and your spirit becomes more alive to God's presence.

This is how revival is sustained. The Spirit who begins the fire also maintains it through prayer.

The Holy Spirit is the power behind every revival prayer meeting, the flame that keeps believers united, and the voice that declares Heaven's will on earth.

"Not by might nor by power, but by My Spirit," says the Lord of hosts."–Zechariah 4:6

And when you pray in the Spirit, you invite revival into your own heart. He is not only the fuel of prayer–He is the fire itself.

PRAYER THAT SHAKES THE EARTH

While God answers the cry of an individual, He moves most powerfully through agreement. When the Church prays in unity, the Heavens open and spiritual strongholds begin to collapse.

Corporate prayer is not about numbers–it's about unity.

"They all continued with one accord in prayer and supplication."–Acts 1:14

The early Church understood this secret. God dwells where His people are united. Disunity quenches revival, but unity attracts it. When believers lay down pride, offense, and personal agendas, their collective prayer becomes a mighty force.

> *"For where two or three are gathered together in My name, I am there in the midst of them."–Matthew 18:20*

Jesus didn't promise to manifest His presence in isolation but in agreement. The power of corporate prayer is not just in what is said but in who is gathered together; believers joined in one Spirit, seeking one outcome: God's will on earth.

There is a dimension of spiritual authority that only manifests when believers pray together in unity. Heaven recognizes agreement because it reflects the heart of God.

> *"Again I say to you that if two of you agree on earth concerning anything that they ask, it will be done for them by My Father in Heaven."–Matthew 18:19*

Agreement does not mean identical words–it means united hearts. When intercessors pray in agreement, their faith multiplies. One person might spark a fire, but a praying church becomes a wildfire.

This is why Satan fights unity–he fears a Church that prays together. When believers stand as one voice ushering in Heaven, the kingdom of hell will be dismantled.

When prayer spreads beyond a few and grips an entire body, a Holy Ghost outpouring is inevitable.

> *"When they had prayed, the place where they were assembled together was shaken."–Acts 4:31*

Corporate prayer changes spiritual climates. It pushes back darkness, releases power, and creates an atmosphere where miracles, signs, wonders become normal. A praying church will become a burning church, and a burning church will become a city set on fire.

Corporate prayer has a way of aligning hearts and keeping the focus on Jesus rather than on personalities.

> *"They continued steadfastly in the apostles' doctrine and fellowship, in the breaking of bread, and in prayers."–Acts 2:42*

The first believers didn't just attend prayer–they continued in it. It was not a special event but a way of life. Prayer meetings were not optional; they were essential and when the Church of Jesus Christ returns to that pattern, revival fire becomes a way of life.

Corporate prayer is more than noise–it is the sound of unity that Heaven recognizes. It's the roar of God's people crying out with one voice. That sound draws the presence of God. That sound confuses the enemy and that sound releases angelic activity.

> *"Behold, how good and how pleasant it is for brethren to dwell*

> *together in unity! ... For there the Lord commanded the blessing."–Psalm 133:1,3*

God commands blessing where unity exists. If a handful of believers can move Heaven together, imagine what happens when entire churches and cities unite in prayer.

The Church was born in a prayer meeting–and it will be revived in one.

Revival cannot be sustained by occasional prayer. It thrives through continual prayer. The great secret of every revivalist was not only how they prayed during public meetings or services but how they lived in conversation with God throughout the day.

> *"Pray without ceasing."–1 Thessalonians 5:17*

Unceasing prayer does not mean constant talking–it means constant awareness.

The early Church prayed in the morning, at noon, and at night. They prayed in persecution, in success, and in suffering. Prayer was not an event. It was their environment.

> *"Continuing daily with one accord in the temple, and breaking bread from house to house, they ate their food with gladness and simplicity of heart."–Acts 2:46*

For them, prayer was the breath of the Spirit within.

UNCEASING PRAYER KEEPS THE FIRE BURNING

Personal fire fades when prayer fades. But when the altar of the heart remains active–when communication with God never ceases–the flame never goes out. It is possible to live in continual revival if you learn to live in continual prayer.

> *"The fire shall ever be burning on the altar; it shall never go out."*–Leviticus 6:13

This altar is not just a physical place–it is your inner life. When your heart stays surrendered, your spirit stays burning. You don't have to wait for Sunday to talk to God. Every moment–at work, in traffic, or at home–can become holy ground.

Enoch's story shows us what a life of unceasing prayer looks like. He didn't pray occasionally, he walked with God daily. His life was a continual fellowship, so deep that one day he simply walked into eternity.

> *"And Enoch walked with God; and he was not, for God took him."*–Genesis 5:24

That's the model of unbroken prayer. To walk with God is to live in continual awareness of His presence. When you walk like that your life becomes a living prayer. Unceasing prayer is not limited to a prayer closet. It means staying connected to God in the midst of everything you do. Every moment can be an offering. The Holy Spirit turns ordinary moments into divine encounters when your heart stays open to Him. The more you practice this, the more natural it becomes. Soon, prayer won't be something you start or a few minutes at the beginning of your day–it will be something you are.

The highest goal of prayer is not power, answers, or results–it is access to God Himself. Prayer is relationship. Prayer is fellowship. Prayer is communication. When you live in continual prayer, you walk in continual access to God.

This is what sustains revival and what Jesus modeled every day.

"He Himself often withdrew into the wilderness and prayed."–Luke 5:16

If Jesus, the Son of God, needed an unbroken connection with the Father, how much more do we? Prayer is not a task to check off–it is the oxygen of the believer's life. Those who learn to live in constant prayer never run dry.

The secret is not in how long you pray, but in how consistently you stay connected. It's a continual exchange–your weakness for His strength, your worry for His peace, and your will for His.

This is what it means to live a life that ignites Heaven daily.

SHAKE HEAVEN AND DISMANTLE HELL

There is a kind of prayer that doesn't whisper through the darkness of this fallen world–it cuts through it. It is not the timid talk of religion but the bold roar of sons and daughters who know their authority. When the redeemed open their mouths under the unction of the Holy Spirit, the atmosphere trembles. Principalities lose their footing. Strongholds collapse. Words, when forged in fire and spoken in faith, become weapons that pierce the veil of darkness. Every declaration drenched in the blood of Jesus carries the authority of Heaven's decree and the sentence of hell's defeat.

This generation must rediscover that kind of praying–the kind that doesn't negotiate with demons but commands them to flee. Prayer is Heaven's invasion point. It is the kingdom of light storming the gates of darkness with the shout of victory already written. The intercessor is not a victim begging for relief; he is a warrior enforcing the dominion Christ already secured. Every time we declare, "Thy Kingdom come," we are driving the flag of Heaven deeper into enemy territory.

Revival prayer does not echo human reasoning–it announces Heaven's plan. It speaks as if the walls have already fallen, as if the captives are already free, and as if awakening is already sweeping through the land. It calls what is not as though it already is, because the authority of Jesus has made it so. This kind of prayer shakes Heaven and dismantles hell.

The Church must rise again–declaring, binding, loosing, and commanding. The gates of hell are not able to withstand a praying people.

Let the people of God lift their voices until the Heavens shake with agreement. Let the earth quake beneath the sound of a people who know the Lion of Judah roars through them. We do not fight for victory, we fight from victory. The enemy is already crushed beneath the feet of Jesus. The blood of Jesus already crushed his head. Every demonic throne is overturned beneath His name. Dominion has already been given. Authority has already been transferred.

Now–declare it. Decree it. Prophesy it and proclaim it until darkness bends its knee and light floods the earth. The shaking is the sound of God's Kingdom advancing in response to the prayers of the saints. The dismantling of hell's Kingdom has begun.

SEVEN
STAND IN HOLY BOLDNESS

"While women weep, as they do now, I'll fight; while little children go hungry, as they do now, I'll fight; while men go to prison, in and out, in and out, as they do now, I'll fight; while there is a drunkard left, while there is a poor lost girl upon the streets, while there remains one dark soul without the light of God, I'll fight–I'll fight to the very end!" –William Booth

THE SPIRIT OF BOLDNESS IN AN AGE OF COWARDICE

There was a time when the sound of the Church shook nations. There was a time when prophets confronted kings and apostles were martyred for calling for religious and political reform.

A time when the gospel was not reduced to entertainment or theory, but was carried on the breath of men and women who knew their God and were convinced and convicted of His message. Their words broke witchcraft, their prayers dismantled empires, and they carried the authority of Heaven. The early believers were not strategists. They were soldiers. They were not public speakers. They were prophets with fire in their bones. The world called them dangerous, but Heaven called them faithful.

A spirit of holy boldness is crying out to be reborn in this generation. We live in an hour where compromise has been disguised as compassion, and fear has been baptized as wisdom. The Church has grown silent in the very moment the world needs her voice. Thankfully the Spirit of the Lion of Judah still fills weak vessels and makes them unbreakable. His fire still turns cowards into conquerors.

Boldness is not a personality trait. It's a spiritual mantle. It is the courage that comes when a man or a woman knows they carry power and authority from God. It is the refusal to retreat when the battle rages. It is the voice that says, "If God is for me, who can be against me?" Holy boldness does not need permission from the world; it moves by the command of Heaven. It rises within sold-out believers in urgent times.

The Book of Acts Church prayed for courage not comfort. They didn't ask for protection. They asked for power. "Grant to Your servants that with all boldness they may speak Your word," they cried and the place where they prayed was shaken. That is not ancient history. It is the blueprint for now. God is raising up a remnant that will once again pray this prayer.

Cowardice is contagious, but so is courage. One voice filled with holy boldness can awaken an army. When David stood before Goliath, the entire nation watched in fear but when he ran toward the battle line, faith exploded in Israel again. The bold act of one man broke the paralysis of thousands. This generation needs preachers who fear God more than social backlash. It needs believers who would rather offend hell than please men. I'm tired of preachers saying they don't want to get political and staying silent. Silence, in times that call for voices of righteousness, is the most "political" response.

The voice of the righteous changes atmospheres and moral climates. It shatters intimidation. It silences the threats of darkness. When a believer opens their mouth under the power of the Holy Spirit, demons are defeated. Every time a child of God declares truth without apology, another chain falls. Every time a believer refuses to compromise, the kingdom of darkness loses ground.

The hour is late. The line between truth and deception has never been clearer. We are surrounded by a culture that mocks righteousness and worships rebellion. But the darker the night, the brighter the light of Christ and His Church must become. This is no time for quiet Christianity. This is no time for hiding behind screens, pews, or a fear of rejection. The Spirit of God is calling His people out of hiding, out of timidity, out of half-hearted living and into holy confrontation.

The sound of the righteous is not a sound of arrogance; it is an announcement of victory. It's the sound of those who've seen The Cross, felt the fire, and refuse to bow to Babylon. It is the sound that declares to hell, "You picked the wrong generation to mess with."

When you've seen the Lamb who was slain standing as the Lion who reigns, you lose the appetite to play it safe. You realize this world is not your home. It's your mission field. You stop whispering about Jesus and start proclaiming Him with fire.

Let the pulpits shake again. Let worship be loud again. Let prayer meetings thunder with war cries again. Let the saints walk into boardrooms, classrooms, and neighborhoods carrying Heaven's authority. Let the sound of the redeemed rise from the streets to the Heavens until every principality hears it: the Church is done being silent.

We were not born to survive in an age of fear. We were born to conquer it and fear nothing but God Himself. And when that sound returns to the Church, no devil, no system, no ideology, and no power of hell will be able to stop what Heaven will unleash.

TAKING A STAND FOR GOD IN A WORLD THAT COMPROMISES

We are living in a time in which culture is asking for surrender, and the world is whispering that silence is safer than truth. This time is separating the spectators from the soldiers. Every generation faces its furnace, and ours is no different. But God has always had a remnant who refuses to bend their knee to the idols of the day. And I prophesy over our generation, "We will not bow."

The world bows quickly, but God looks for those who stand firm in the fire. True boldness is not born on mountaintops of victory. No, it is forged in valleys of adversity. That kind of conviction refuses to bend under the weight of cultural approval. It is the courage that says, "Even if I stand alone, I will not sacrifice conviction on the altar of approval."

When Daniel was told that no man could pray to any god but the king, he didn't retreat or negotiate. Scripture says, *"He knelt down on his knees three times that day, and prayed and gave thanks before his God, as was his custom since early days"* (Daniel 6:10). His faith was steadfast. His prayer wasn't hidden, it was defiant. The lions' den did not break him. It revealed God. God shut the mouths of beasts to testify that faith still conquers fear.

In the same way, Shadrach, Meshach, and Abednego stood when all others bowed. They didn't calculate outcomes or wait for permission. Their response to Nebuchadnezzar was unshakable:

> *"We do not serve your gods, nor will we worship the golden image which you have set up... and even if our God does not deliver us, we will not bow"–Daniel 3:18*

They didn't compromise to save themselves. They stood to glorify God. And when they were thrown into the flames, the fire that should have consumed them became the place where the Son of God walked beside them. Their boldness exposed the emptiness of the world's power and revealed the fourth Man in the fire.

Elijah faced the same test when Israel bowed to Baal. On Mount Carmel, he confronted the prophets of deception and declared before the nation, *"How long will you falter between two opinions? If the Lord is God, follow Him"* (1 Kings 18:21). Surrounded, outnumbered, and mocked, Elijah stood and fire answered his faith.

This is what it means to take a stand for God in a compromising world. It means confronting deception, even when it costs you acceptance. It means standing for righteousness, even when the world labels it hate. It means refusing to water down the gospel for the approval of men.

Our age has its own idols: moral confusion, self-worship, greed, perversion, and political ideologies that defy the Word of God. The furnace now burns in the form of public shaming, social rejection, and cultural exile. But the command of Heaven remains the same—stand.

You can never fight darkness by agreeing with it. You can never defeat deception by remaining quiet about it. The moment you decide to take a stand, you draw the line where Heaven and hell divide. Boldness is not the absence of fear, it's the mastery of fear through faith.

Taking a stand for God is not rebellion against man. It's obedience to God and His Word. It's saying, "If I must be misunderstood, let it be for truth's sake. If I must lose something, let it be for His glory." Every stand taken in righteousness gets Heaven's attention. When believers of Jesus refuse to bow, God sends angels. And when we hold the line, fire falls again.

This is the moment for the Church to stop bowing to opinion polls and start standing on the Word of God. The Spirit of compromise must be confronted, and the spirit of boldness must rise. When God finds people who will not bow, He will once again reveal His glory to a generation that has forgotten His power.

So stand firm. Stand when the pressure increases. Stand when fear tempts you to hide. Stand when others walk away. Because the God who stood with Daniel, who walked with the three in the fire, and who answered Elijah with flames, will stand with you.

You are not outnumbered. You are backed by Heaven.

THE WAR AGAINST POWERLESS CHRISTIANITY

There is a faith that sings but never shakes hell. A belief that lifts its hands but never lifts its sword. It smiles at sin and it blesses compromise. It fills buildings but leaves souls bound and lost. This is the counterfeit Christianity of our generation– a gospel drained of confrontation, a cross stripped of sacrifice, and a Spirit replaced by good marketing. It is time for it to fall.

Powerless religion is the enemy of revival. It says the right words but carries no weight. It quotes Scripture but denies its authority. It preaches positivity when God is demanding holiness. The apostle Paul warned of this day: *"Having a form of godliness but denying its power. And from such people turn away" (2 Timothy 3:5).* That verse is not about unbelievers, it's about pulpits that have forgotten Pentecost.

When Jesus walked into the temple and found merchants instead of ministers, He didn't hold a seminar, He made a whip. He drove out the corruption. And holy fire is rising again in this generation. The Church was not meant to entertain or conform to the world but to confront it with truth and power. If the early disciples preached what many preach today, they would have been applauded, not persecuted.

Where there is no power, there is no transformation. When Peter and John stood before the Sanhedrin, accused of healing the crippled man, Scripture says, *"When they saw the boldness of Peter and John, and perceived that they were uneducated and untrained men, they marveled; and they realized that they had been with Jesus" (Acts 4:13).* That's the difference–being with Jesus produces power that cannot be taught, only caught.

Powerless Christianity offers therapy when deliverance is needed. I am convinced the Church of Jesus Christ has traded altars for therapy couches. And instead of producing healed, strong, and whole saints, we have entitled, critical, and bound victims. Powerless Christianity offers motivation when demons must be cast out. It offers self-help when The Cross asks for self-denial. This counterfeit gospel leads to larger crowds but the real gospel leads to crucifixion. It doesn't produce fame, it promises persecution. And in that persecution, God is revealed.

Look at Paul on the island of Malta. When the viper latched onto his hand, the people waited for him to die, but he shook the creature into the fire and kept preaching (Acts 28:3-6). That is what authentic power looks like. It doesn't flinch under attack. It endures. It doesn't fear the venom of this world, it carries the power and healing of Heaven.

Churches that overcome this counterfeit gospel will be churches with upper room DNA. A DNA of fire that turns weak men into witnesses. Until the Spirit once again fills the tabernacles of our churches, we will keep producing empty noise without any change.

But God is calling His people to confront the counterfeit.

To challenge messages that dilute holiness and cheapen grace. To reject platforms built on personality rather than presence. To expose doctrines that pacify the flesh while starving the spirit. The time for dead, empty, status quo Christianity has expired. Heaven is pouring out power that heals the sick, raises the dead, casts out devils, and shakes cities awake and His people must position themselves to receive it.

Let me be clear: the war against powerless Christianity is not about frustration toward people. We are not called to attack the Church. We are called to awaken it. We are the generation that has to rebuild the altar. We are the generation that has to repair the breach and raise the standard. We must get the Word back in the pulpit, the Blood back in our sermons, and the Breath of the Holy Ghost back in our tabernacles. When that happens, the counterfeit will crumble under the weight of a real move of God.

So reject empty, powerless Christianity and let the real power of God flow again. The Church is alive, and Christ still reigns.

SHATTERING THE SILENCE—SPEAKING UP FOR GOD IN A GODLESS SOCIETY

It has been clear to me for several years that there is a demonic silence attempting to muzzle this generation. It creeps into pulpits, classrooms, and conversations—pressuring believers to compromise their convictions for tolerance. The spirit of this age says, "Be quiet about your faith. Keep your truth to yourself." But the gospel was meant to be declared and not whispered. The gospel is confrontational. The gospel isn't supposed to stay in church basements and private bible studies. It is meant to confront. It is meant to offend. It was not made for safety. The Word became flash and they nailed Him to a tree.

Jesus said plainly, *"Whoever is ashamed of Me and My words, the Son of Man will be ashamed of him when He comes in His own glory" (Luke 9:26).* What a warning!

The enemy wants us to soften this message but Jesus didn't whisper. He preached in temples, on hillsides, in courtrooms, and at dinner tables. And when they told Him to be quiet, He picked up a cross. Not a symbolic one, a real one. Heavy. Bloody. Splintered.

When Peter stood on the Day of Pentecost before thousands who had crucified the Lord, he preached with conviction: *"This Jesus whom you crucified, God has made both Lord and Christ" (Acts 2:36).* The same crowd that mocked them became the crowd that repented at Peter's words. Why? Because one man refused to be silent.

You are called to something stronger than silence. Don't ever let fear become your theology. Boldness is the mark of people who truly know God. In Acts chapter 4, when the apostles were threatened not to speak in the name of Jesus, they too answered with conviction: *"Whether it is right in the sight of God to listen to you more than to God, you judge. For we cannot but speak the things which we have seen and heard"* (Acts 4:19–20).

But today, the enemy has convinced many believers that silence is safer. That being neutral is the more noble thing to be. But neutrality is never neutral. It always favors the oppressor and when truth is silenced, lies reign. When righteousness is quiet, wickedness increases. Satan doesn't need to destroy a generation if he can just keep the saints quiet long enough for darkness to become normal.

The prophets of old didn't have microphones, social media, or platforms, but they did have fire in their bones. Jeremiah cried, *"His word was in my heart like a burning fire shut up in my bones; I was weary of holding it back, and I could not"* (Jeremiah 20:9). That fire has returned to the Church again. We don't conform the message of The Cross to fit the culture of the times. We proclaim it until the culture repents and comes to Christ.

In a world that mocks the truth and celebrates everything ungodly, we cannot afford to remain silent. Silence is partnership with darkness. But when a believer speaks up for righteousness, light pushes back against the darkness. Every time you stand in truth at your workplace, school, or home, you are drawing a line the enemy cannot cross.

Paul wrote, *"I am not ashamed of the gospel of Christ, for it is the power of God to salvation for everyone who believes"* (Romans 1:16). The gospel is not an opinion to be debated, it is a living truth that demands a response. We are not salesmen trying to persuade people to like God. We are ambassadors sent to represent Him with power, conviction, and authority.

Don't whisper about Jesus. Don't worry about offending others with your faith. Lift your voice like a trumpet and declare Christ as the only hope for a dying world. The spirit of fear that silences believers must be broken. The days of quiet Christianity are over. We are Heaven's voice in an hour of confusion, God's trumpet in a culture of compromise, and Christ's messengers in a time of moral chaos.

You are not supposed to fit in. You were born again to stand out. The Church of Acts didn't survive by silence. She overcame by testimony and truth. Scripture declares, *"They overcame him by the blood of the Lamb and by the word of their testimony, and they did not love their lives to the death" (Revelation 12:11).*

This is what it means to shatter the silence–to open your mouth when others refuse, to speak life where death has taken hold, and to declare the Kingdom of God on earth when the world denies it. The sound of your voice becomes a strike against the gates of hell.

Let the people of God rise again with unfiltered truth in their mouths. Let the pulpits shake with the Word of God again. Let believers flood social spaces with truth, testimony, and an unashamed declaration that Jesus Christ died, was buried and rose again on the third day to save us from our sins. Because when the Church finally breaks her silence, the world will remember that Jesus still lives and Heaven still has a voice, and it speaks through those who fear God more than man.

THE CLASH OF KINGDOMS– CONFRONTING THE CULTURE AND THE DOCTRINES OF DEMONS

It is evident that light has collided with darkness in our time–two kingdoms warring for the soul of a generation. The culture we see unraveling before our eyes is not random. It is strategic. The confusion in identity, the political corruption, the celebration of sin–these are not social trends. They are part of a strategic, spiritual war. Behind the headlines are principalities, ancient spirits waging war against God. What we are witnessing is not cultural decay–it is demonic warfare dressed in modern language.

Paul wrote, *"We do not wrestle against flesh and blood, but against principalities, against powers, against the rulers of the darkness of this age, against spiritual hosts of wickedness in the heavenly places"* (Ephesians 6:12). Paul's language isn't metaphorical. It is the reality the Church has forgotten. The battleground is not just in governments and schools, it is in minds, it is in the media, and it is in every social structure that makes up this world. Doctrines of demons are no longer hidden in temples. They are streamed into homes, taught in classrooms, and preached from so-called religious platforms.

Satan has always used deception to destroy nations. He has no new tricks–only old lies in modern packages. From the garden to this present day, his strategy has been the same: twist God's word, confuse identity, and promise freedom that leads to bondage. In Eden, he whispered, "You will be like God." Today, he whispers, "You are your own god." It is the same rebellion wearing a modern face.

When Paul warned Timothy about the last days, he described them perfectly:

"The Spirit expressly says that in latter times some will depart from the faith, giving heed to deceiving spirits and doctrines of demons" (1 Timothy 4:1).

We are there now. The doctrines of demons are not only alive, they are being legislated and normalized. Lies about gender, family, morality, and truth itself are being celebrated with zeal. Evil no longer hides. It advertises with majority acceptance. Thank God, in the midst of this darkness, God is raising up voices that carry the light of Christ and the holy boldness to confront.

The Church won't win this war with diplomacy. We are not called to negotiate with the devil. We are called to have dominion over him. Darkness does not yield to negotiation but it will flee from a believer's authority. When Elijah stood on Mount Carmel, he didn't blend his message with Baal's prophets. He confronted them. He drew a line and said, "If the Lord is God, follow Him." Fire fell on an altar where compromise did not have a chance to live. That holy confrontation has awakened in the Church again.

This is the clash of kingdoms–truth versus deception, light versus darkness, righteousness versus rebellion. You can't embrace both. Jesus said, *"He who is not with Me is against Me" (Matthew 12:30)*. There is no middle ground in a war for the souls of mankind.

Hell has launched an all-out assault on truth. It has targeted children with confusion. It has divided families and it has attempted to distract the Church. But the Remnant Church of Jesus Christ is not retreating. The Spirit of God is calling for sold out ones; warriors who will not surrender or back down. They will preach Christ, confront sin without apology, and stand for truth even if it costs them everything.

The confrontation isn't about anger–it's about covenant loyalty. The Church does not hate the world. The Church is burdened for the world and refuses to let it remain enslaved. To confront deception is to love deeply enough to tell the truth. Jesus didn't come to coexist with darkness; He came to destroy the works of the devil (1 John 3:8).

This is why boldness is essential in this hour. We don't need more agreeable Christians, we need unshakable ones. We need believers who understand that tolerance is not love when it tolerates what destroys people's souls. Real love confronts. Godly love tells the truth even when it hurts. The love of Christ shines a light into the pit and pulls people out, no matter the cost.

It is so important that we learn to discern the spirits at work behind the systems. The agendas that shape entertainment, education, and politics are not neutral. They are spiritual. The push to normalize sin, blur the lines of gender, and deconstruct infallible gospel truth is demonic at its root. And the Church of Jesus Christ can't afford to stand by and watch quietly while hell attempts to destroy the next generation.

We need more preaching that exposes darkness, more intercession that pulls down strongholds, and more believers who walk into demonic systems with the authority of The Cross and dismantle them. We were not plucked out of eternity and placed on the earth for such a time as this to survive it. We were placed here to disrupt it. The Kingdom of God does not conform to the culture–it invades it.

I say, we declare, once again, *"The kingdoms of this world have become the Kingdoms of our Lord and of His Christ" (Revelation 11:15)*. That is the mandate of the hour we are living in. We are God's invasion force to reclaim all that the enemy has stolen. Expose the lies. Speak the truth. Cast down the doctrines of demons and replace them with the gospel of power. The Cross still stands. The Blood still works. The Tomb is still empty. The gospel has not lost one ounce of power and as long as believers refuse to bow, the gates of hell will continue to fall.

THE BATTLE FOR THE BLOODLINE— TAKING A STAND FOR OUR CHILDREN AND THE NEXT GENERATION

We are in a spiritual war for the next generation. This battle is visible, horrific, and intentional. The target is the bloodline. The assault is demonic. The enemy has set his sights on the sons and daughters of this generation, and he is using the same ancient spirits that demanded the blood of the innocent in ages past. The altars of Molech have not disappeared but they have been modernized. What was once done in shadows is now defended in courts and celebrated in streets.

Hell's thirst for blood is as real now as it was in the days of Israel's rebellion. The spirit that demanded children to be passed through fire then is behind the killing of the unborn today. Abortion is not just a social issue or a political debate. It is a demonic ritual hidden under the strategic language of "choice." It is child sacrifice to the gods of convenience and self-worship. It is the modern temple of Molech built on lies and legal justification.

When Pharaoh feared the rise of deliverers, he slaughtered Hebrew sons. When Herod feared the birth of the Messiah, he ordered the massacre of infants. Every time God intends to birth deliverance, hell tries to kill it before it can be born. And in our day, millions of voices have been silenced before they could ever even cry; before they could speak, and before they could fulfill their calling. This is not progress. It is a demonic war.

But just as God preserved Moses in a basket and Jesus in a manger, He is preserving destinies that hell can't touch. He is raising up a generation of intercessors, mothers, fathers, and leaders who will not stand by while the innocent are destroyed. We are a voice for the voiceless. Proverbs 31:8–9 commands, *"Open your mouth for the speechless, in the cause of all who are appointed to die. Open your mouth, judge righteously, and plead the cause of the poor and needy."*

The shedding of innocent blood brings judgment on nations. Scripture says, *"They shed innocent blood, the blood of their sons and daughters... and the land was defiled with blood"* (Psalm 106:38). On this subject, scripture is clear: your silence is agreement and your compromise is participation. If the Church refuses to confront this evil, we will be held accountable for the blood that cries out from the ground.

But I am not trying to give you a message of despair. My goal is a call to arms. God raises deliverers in dark times. The Holy Spirit is moving on this generation of believers to protect the unborn, to intercede for mothers, and to break the demonic altars that have claimed too many lives. Nehemiah's cry must become our cry: *"Fight for your brethren, your sons, your daughters, your wives, and your houses"* (Nehemiah 4:14). The wall-builders of this hour are parents, pastors, intercessors, and warriors who refuse to allow another generation to be destroyed by this deception.

This is also a call to repentance and redemption. The mercy of God runs deeper than sin, and The Cross of Christ is still powerful enough to heal every wound. For anyone who has walked through the pain of abortion, hear this: Jesus does not condemn you. His blood restores what was lost and redeems what was taken. What the enemy meant for destruction, God can still turn into testimony. But the Church must speak the truth boldly so healing can begin.

The war for the next generation goes beyond the womb. It reaches into schools, media, identity, and morality. The spirits that kill in infancy seek to corrupt in adolescence. The agenda to confuse gender, blur family, and distort truth is part of the same demonic scheme to destroy what God has created. But those who stand with God will stand victorious.

Joshua's words still stand: *"As for me and my house, we will serve the Lord" (Joshua 24:15)*. His words were a declaration of war against every false god and against a corrupt culture. Every family must now choose whom they will serve just as in Joshua's day.

The Church must once again become the defender of life–not just in policy, but in power. We must pray for an awakening of conscience and conviction. We must be both the voice and the hands of Christ–preaching life, rescuing the unborn, and restoring the broken.

The next generation will not be surrendered to the systems of Babylon. We will not bow to the altars of Molech. We will not allow death to define our culture. We will take our stand until the blood cries of the innocent are answered by a blood-covered Church that stands in righteousness and intercession.

This battle for the bloodline is a defining fight in our generation that we are called to win. Let every believer rise as a defender of destiny. Let every church become a sanctuary for life. Let every father, mother, and saint stand in the gap until the demonic altars of abortion crumble under the weight of revival and the fear of the Lord fills the land again.

Because this time, Pharaoh will fail. Herod will fall. Molech will be silenced. And the children, born and unborn, will live to carry the fire of revival that no power of hell can extinguish.

We are not raising survivors. We are raising soldiers. We are not building safe spaces. We are building sanctuaries of power. The call is to train them, arm them, and release them. *"Out of the mouth of babes and nursing infants You have ordained strength, because of Your enemies, that You may silence the enemy and the avenger"* (Psalm 8:2). Even the youngest carry God's authority when they know their identity.

The enemy trembles at what this next generation will become if we refuse to compromise. There are Davids waiting to slay giants, Esthers called to rescue nations, Josiahs destined to tear down altars of idolatry. The future fires of revival are not going to burn through famous names. They are going to come through the sons and daughters who will burn brighter than their predecessors because someone fought for them.

So stand your ground. Guard your home. Speak truth when the world lies. Pray for your children. Surround them in fire. Teach them Scripture. Show them miracles. Let them see that Jesus is not a story, they can feel His fire. Don't just play dress-up on Sundays; be the Church, in front of them, every day. Live the gospel because your life is preaching the loudest to them. We will not lose our sons. We will not lose our daughters. We will not watch in silence as the enemy poisons their minds and steals their purpose. This is our watch. This is our fight. And as long as there is breath in our lungs and the Spirit of God within us, the bloodline will be redeemed, the next generation will rise, and the name of Jesus will be declared across their lips with unshakable power.

PREACHING THE GOSPEL WITH UNCOMPROMISING POWER

The battlefield of our time is not in some distant land. It's right where we stand. Every workplace, every neighborhood, and every home has become ground in the war for souls. The greatest act of warfare you can commit is to open your mouth and proclaim the gospel of Jesus Christ with fire, without apology, and without fear.

Paul said, *"For I am not ashamed of the gospel of Christ, for it is the power of God to salvation for everyone who believes"* *(Romans 1:16)*. That word power, dunamis, means an explosive, earth-shaking force. When the gospel is preached in full authority, souls will be saved.

In Acts 17, it was said of the early believers, "These who have turned the world upside down have come here too." They were accused of upheaval because they carried a spirit of revolution. They didn't just share an opinion, they carried a kingdom. Everywhere they went, idolatry fell, sorcery was exposed, and whole cities were shaken. That's the fire that belongs to us. The same Holy Spirit that anointed Jesus to *"preach the gospel to the poor... heal the brokenhearted... proclaim liberty to the captives" (Luke 4:18)* rests upon the sons and daughters of God today.

Anointed, uncompromising preaching doesn't adjust the Word to fit the listener, it reaches into the soul of the listener and convicts them to align with the Word. It challenges them to repentance and it is full of conviction. When Peter preached at Pentecost, his words pierced hearts, and three thousand were added to the Church in a single day. The same sword that cut them was the one that healed them. Truth pierces and wounds before it saves.

Every believer is called to be a frontline preacher. You don't need a pulpit, you just need willingness, a voice, and obedience. When you share your testimony, you confront the kingdom of darkness. When you pray for the sick, the enemy loses ground. Every time you cast out a demon, you enforce the victory of Calvary. Jesus said, *"These signs will follow those who believe: In My name they will cast out demons... they will lay hands on the sick, and they will recover"* (Mark 16:17-18). That was not just for the pages of your bible. It was for us today. God does miracles NOW!

The enemy has convinced many that the supernatural ended with the apostles, but that is not what the Bible says. The power that fell in Acts has never left the Church. It only left the comfortable. It only left those who refused its downpour. It only left those content to live without it. Miracles are not our history. They are the normal operation of a Church filled with the Holy Ghost. The same Spirit that raised Jesus from the dead still flows through believers who dare to act on what they believe.

Evangelistic fires are burning again. The fields are white, and the harvest is massive, but the laborers must go. Street corners, prisons, schools, hospitals, stadiums, boardrooms, and digital platforms are waiting for carriers of the flame. Jesus already commanded, *"Go into all the world."* When you go, you don't go alone. Jesus backs every step taken in obedience.

The lost souls of mankind don't need empty words. They need voices clothed in power; men and women who preach the truth, who lay hands on the sick without hesitation, who declare freedom to captives, and who refuse to back down. Saints of God aren't background people. We are frontline people. We face the darkness with light, we confront evil with authority, and we preach Christ until the moral climate of a city changes.

Let your words become weapons and don't edit the gospel for comfort or applause. You carry the same Holy Ghost that set nations on fire through fishermen, tax collectors, and former prisoners. Preach until hearts burn. Preach until devils flee. Preach until the sick rise. Preach until this generation knows that the gospel is not a story, it is a living and eternal truth. You are not waiting for revival. You are carrying it. And when you step onto the field, every demon will know that the frontlines have been taken back by the sons and daughters of God.

SPIRITUAL WARFARE AND THE AUTHORITY OF THE BELIEVER

The war that is raging is beyond what the natural eyes can see, and every believer is drafted into it. This is a spiritual reality. Whether we fight or not, the enemy is already fighting. But the truth is the enemy is fighting on a battlefield that God has armed His people to dominate. The Church of Jesus Christ is not a defensive entity, we are a conquering army. We don't run from devils. We drive them out.

The Word of God makes this clear: *"For the weapons of our warfare are not carnal but mighty in God for pulling down strongholds" (2 Corinthians 10:4).* We have been given spiritual weapons capable of demolishing demonic systems, dismantling lies, and disarming the kingdom of darkness. The problem is not a lack of power. It is a lack of awareness. Too many saints live like civilians when they were born to be soldiers.

The authority of the believer is not self-confidence, it is delegated power given to us by God. When Jesus said, "Behold, I give you authority to trample on serpents and scorpions, and over all the power of the enemy" (Luke 10:19), He was not exaggerating. That word authority–exousia–means delegated power, the legal right to act on Heaven's behalf. You carry the King's signature in the Spirit. You do not pray hoping for victory. You pray from victory already won.

Hell can't defeat the authority of a believer. But demons recognize who has been with Jesus and who merely talks about Him. In Acts 19, the sons of Sceva tried to use Jesus' name without submission to His Lordship and the demons tore them apart. Authority flows only from relationship. And you can't cast out what you secretly entertain. You can't rebuke darkness while making peace with it. True authority is exercised in holiness and obedience.

Ephesians 6 commands us to "put on the whole armor of God." Each piece is not symbolic; it is literal, spiritual weaponry. The belt of truth secures your stability. The breastplate of righteousness guards your heart from condemnation. The shoes of peace give you ground to stand in hostile territory. The shield of faith extinguishes the fiery darts of doubt and fear. The helmet of salvation protects your mind from deception. And the sword of the Spirit, which is the Word of God, gives you the power to strike back.

When Jesus faced Satan in the wilderness, He didn't argue. He declared, "It is written." The Word was His weapon. The devil cannot be reasoned with, he must be resisted. And he only flees from those who are submitted to God and fight back with Scripture, not opinion. Every believer must learn to swing the sword with accuracy and to declare the Word of God with power.

Spiritual warfare is continual. The enemy's goal is not just to attack you but to wear you down. That's why Paul said, *"Having done all, to stand" (Ephesians 6:13)*. Standing is not weakness, it's warfare. It means holding your ground, refusing to retreat, and planting your feet in the victory Christ already secured. The devil's power is built on deception, and the moment you stop believing his lies, his stronghold collapses.

Believers should not be reacting to the devil. We should be resisting him.

When the righteous decree a thing, it shall be established. When the saints command in the name of Jesus, hell's assignments are canceled. Never forget that the devil is a defeated foe. His head was crushed at Calvary and his authority was stripped. His keys were already taken by the risen Christ. You are not fighting for victory. You are enforcing victory. You are not trying to win. You are reminding hell that it has already lost.

Take up your sword. Open your mouth and strike with Scripture. Bind the spirit of fear. Break the chains of oppression. Rebuke sickness. Cast out demons. Declare truth. Do not fight like a victim, fight like a victor. The powers of darkness flee when you stand in your authority as a blood-bought believer of Jesus Christ.

The battlefield belongs to the bold. The war is already won. Now stand.

NO MORE SPECTATORS–BREAKING FREE FROM PASSIVE CHRISTIANITY

The modern Church has become filled with spectators, watchers, observers, and critics; people who sit in the stands while a few do the fighting on the field. But the Kingdom of God is not a movie theater. It's a battlefield. There are no reclining seats in the army of the Lord, only frontlines. And we weren't saved to sit. We were saved to serve, to war, and to win.

Jesus said, "Follow Me." not, "Come and watch Me." That call is a call to continue His mission until He returns. The early Church understood this. It wasn't built by professionals or brilliant, successful people. It was built by fishermen, and tax collectors, and former prisoners, and ordinary believers who understood that the power of God was available for every believer. They understood that they all carried fire and every disciple could operate in God's authority.

Passive Christianity is one of the greatest plagues of our time. It's a quiet surrender that looks like politeness but smells like death. It looks alive but it is dead. It hides behind excuses, passes off responsibility to others, and disguises cowardice as humility. The gospel demands that we engage. The gospel demands action. Scripture commands, "Be doers of the word, and not hearers only, deceiving yourselves" (James 1:22).

The Church isn't a gathering of spectators who watch a few anointed people perform. The early church didn't just assemble together, they were the Church. They met in homes, broke bread, prayed, and turned cities upside down. Every street became a place where the fire of God could pour out. Every conversation became a mission field. They understood something we've forgotten: revival doesn't come through faithful attendance. Revival comes through burning, radical obedience.

Elijah didn't wait for someone else to confront Ahab. David didn't wait for Saul to face Goliath. Esther didn't wait for another woman to go before the king. They stepped out when others hesitated and history was rewritten through their courage. The Church is rediscovering this same spirit. We cannot wait for another evangelist, another conference, or another revival event. The spirit of revival is inside of us and it's time for it to erupt and spread.

Too many believers have become analysts who critique moves of God instead of joining them. They debate theology while demons terrorize cities. They spectate while others bleed on the battlefield. Instead they should be positioning themselves under the flow of God's glory, winning souls, casting out devils and taking their place in the Battle of the Ages; the battle between light and darkness for the souls of mankind.

But praise the Lord, He is shaking the Church again, calling every believer back to the frontlines because there is no neutral ground. There are no sideline saints. Every believer is either advancing the kingdom or allowing darkness to advance unchecked.

The apostle Paul wrote, *"Do you not know that those who run in a race all run, but one receives the prize? Run in such a way that you may obtain it"* (1 Corinthians 9:24). Christianity isn't meant to be lived sitting down. The call is to run, to contend, to labor, and to fight for the faith. There is no participation trophy in the Kingdom of God, only a crown for those who finish their race well. The Holy Spirit is igniting a new boldness in believers who have grown weary of comfort. He is awakening evangelists in workplaces, prophets in classrooms, intercessors in boardrooms, and warriors in living rooms. The Spirit is raising up men and women who will say, "Put me in, Lord, I'm done watching."

We have watched the world and the devil mock holiness, redefine love, and try to silence truth. We've watched souls slip into eternity while the Church slept or fought and debated about our preferences. Enough. It's time for unity and action. It's time to spread the gospel in power, at a greater rate than ever before.

Every believer has a sword, every believer has authority, and every believer has a mandate. Shake off apathy and engage. Don't watch the war, wage it. Your prayers matter. Your voice matters. Your obedience matters. You have a role to play, a weapon to wield, territory to claim, and King Jesus to represent.

Hell fears a fully awakened Body, united in purpose, unafraid of pain, and unstoppable in mission. The battle is already raging. The only question is: will you watch it, or will you fight it?

FEARLESS UNTIL THE FINISH–STANDING WHEN THE WORLD SHAKES

Scripture says, *"See that you are not troubled; for all these things must come to pass"* (Matthew 24:6). Jesus didn't promise it would be easy but He did promise victory. The shaking is not our downfall, it is our proving ground. And every shaking exposes what cannot be shaken: the unbreakable kingdom inside of us.

False foundations are crumbling–political, cultural, and religious. The world's confidence is built on sand, but the Church stands on the Rock. When the troubles of this world rise, we do not retreat in fear. We plant our feet deeper in truth. We don't have panic in our eyes, we have prophecy in our mouths. The shaking is not a sign that we are losing. It's the sound of hell's structures collapsing.

The Spirit of God is forging an army that cannot be intimidated. Jesus is coming back for a victorious bride not a victimized, fear-filled one. Fear has no hold on those who know eternity. Paul wrote, *"None of these things move me; nor do I count my life dear to myself, so that I may finish my race with joy" (Acts 20:24).* That's the spirit of the end-time believer. Our eyes are fixed on eternity, our hearts are steady, and our spirits are unyielding.

The Holy Spirit is our strength and He will carry us through the final shaking.

There is a holy fearlessness that only comes from standing close to the throne. When the Lion of Judah lives inside of you, timidity dies. When The Cross is your identity, death loses its sting. Fear cannot survive in the presence of fire. That's why the enemy attacks with intimidation because he knows a fearless Church is an unstoppable one.

Hell fears a believer who says, "I will not bend, I will not break, I will not back down." The martyrs of the past are our reminders. They stood when empires threatened, they sang in prisons, they shone with the faces of angels while being stoned, and they burned with joy on the stakes of persecution. Their blood still speaks today, declaring to this generation: "Fear nothing. Finish strong."

The Church is not losing. It's awakening. The shaking is not our defeat. It's our commissioning. God is raising up men and women who see fear as an opportunity for faith and persecution as the price of true dominion.

Do not be moved by what you see. Heaven is still ruling. The throne is still occupied. The Lamb has already triumphed. You are not on the losing side of history. You are the enforcement of a finished victory. The King is returning, and until He does, we stand, blood-washed, Spirit-filled, battle-ready, and unafraid.

The words of Joshua echo through this generation as a prophetic mandate:

> *"Be strong and courageous. Do not be afraid or dismayed, for the Lord your God is with you wherever you go" (Joshua 1:9).*

When the dust settles, the fearful will have fled, the faithless will have fallen, but the faithful will still be standing–clothed in glory, crowned with fire, and fearless.

Unashamed. Uncompromising. Unafraid.

Standing tall in the storm, declaring to the powers of hell, "We will not move, We will not bow, We will burn until the end."

EIGHT
BECOME A TORCH OF REVIVAL FIRE

"Most Christians would like to send their recruits to Bible college for five years; I would like to send them to hell for five minutes. That would do more than anything else to prepare them for a lifetime of compassionate ministry." –William Booth

"I plant one foot in hell and the other in eternity and I snatch as many souls from the burning as I possibly can." –John Wesley

"If sinners will be damned at least let them leap to hell over our bodies and if they will perish let them perish with our arms about their knees begging them not to go there. If hell must be filled at least let it be filled in the teeth of our exertions and let not one go there unwarned or unprayed for." –Charles Spurgeon

HEAVEN'S MANDATE FOR THE LAST HOUR

There is a sound echoing through the Heavens from the throne of God. It is not a call for the sophisticated or the well-known, not for the cautious or the gifted. It is a call for those who will burn. God is searching for men and women who will yield to His fire until everything temporal is consumed and only eternal purpose remains. The Holy Spirit is lighting torches in ordinary hearts to ignite extraordinary moves of God.

Every revival in history began with fire from above meeting flesh willing to burn below. When God wants to awaken a generation, He sets His people on fire with inescapable purpose and a flame of urgency directly from Heaven.

This is His pattern. When God's fire falls, it never falls just to fall or just for a temporary blessing. It falls for sending. And you, blood-bought believer of Jesus Christ, are being sent into a Godless society that has forgotten its Creator.

To burn for God is to let Him consume every lesser affection. It means your dreams, your reputation, your comfort, and your control are all laid on the altar until nothing remains but obedience. The flames that once rested on altars of sacrifice now burn in human hearts. You are the lamp. He is the flame. The world grows darker by the hour, but God's answer hasn't changed–it is fire.

Moses saw it on the backside of the desert–a bush engulfed in flames but not consumed (Exodus 3:2). God was revealing His nature to a weary man running from his calling. The fire burned, but the bush lived. That was the message: "If you let Me burn in you, I will not destroy you–I will display Myself through you."

The fire of God will either purify you now or judge you later. There are only two fires, the fires of revival and the fires of judgment. It is far better to burn now in surrender than to burn later in separation. Revival fire is mercy's last call before the fire of eternity consumes all rebellion.

The call to burn is personal. It's a call from Jesus Christ to each individual believer and the Lord is still asking, "Who will let Me light them on fire?" The eyes of the Lord scan the earth looking for those whose hearts are flammable. This is Heaven's mandate for the last hour: Burn until the darkness breaks.

Let your life become the match that sets others on fire. There is a generation drowning in deception and waiting for someone to ignite truth again. The world's darkness is thick, but the fire from the throne of God overcomes it with ease.

BETWEEN TWO FIRES–REVIVAL FIRE OR JUDGMENT FIRE

Every generation stands between two flames–the fire that revives and the fire that judges. One refines and the other destroys. One burns with eternal love and the other burns with eternal loss.

And the Church, the blood-bought sons and daughters of the Living God, has been placed in the middle of these two fires. We have not been placed here as bystanders. We have been placed here as rescuers.

The world is rushing toward eternal fire, and God has placed torches in our hands. We are the line between God's mercy and eternal separation. When revival fire burns in us, it becomes the flame that pulls others from the coming judgment. Every believer who carries the fire of God becomes a bridge between the flames lighting the way to salvation before it's too late. The hour is urgent. Time is running out. Jesus is coming soon.

Jesus didn't talk about hell to terrify the redeemed. He spoke of hell to compel them and to awaken them. He described it so vividly that those who believe would never forget the cost of a soul. Hell is not an imaginary place. It is the final destination of those who reject Jesus and His sacrifice on The Cross of Calvary. It is the most devastating reality in the universe: an eternal separation from the presence of God, a place without grace, without light, without hope, and without escape. Jesus said it was *"prepared for the devil and his angels" (Matthew 25:41)*. Hell was not meant for humanity but every soul that rejects Christ will share the destiny of the one they chose to follow instead of Christ.

Imagine it: a place where the mind never forgets, the

body never dies, and the heart never stops yearning for the chance that never comes. The fires of hell do not consume; instead they torment. The worm does not die, it gnaws. The darkness does not hide, it suffocates. It is eternal regret without any remedy–forever remembering every sermon ignored, every prayer rejected, and every invitation to receive salvation in Christ denied.

But as horrifying as hell is, the greater tragedy is that people are heading there unwarned. Many people must still hear that there is a Savior who died to spare them from that place. Others have heard but have never seen the fire of conviction burning in a believer's life strongly enough to make them listen. That is where you come in.

Believers are set on fire with the fire of God to light the path for those stumbling toward the edge of eternity. The flame that burns within you is not for display. It's for deliverance. Every soul around you is an eternal being who will spend forever in Heaven or hell. When revival fire grips your life, you stop seeing people as faces in a crowd and you start seeing them as souls to be rescued from a greater fire.

When the rich man in Luke 16 lifted his eyes in torment, his first thought was for his brothers still alive on earth. *"I beg you, Father, send someone to warn them," he cried (Luke 16:27–28)*. Even from hell, his only plea was for a preacher. His urgency echoes through time: "Warn them before it's too late!" That cry is the cry of everyone who burns for Jesus, "I must warn them before it's too late!"

We do not preach, witness, or serve to earn God's favor. We do it because we have felt His fire and we have seen what is ahead of those who refuse it. The reality of hell should break our hearts, not harden them. The idea that every second someone somewhere is going to that place for all eternity should compel us to action. Revival fire is not for entertainment. It's a fire that rescues from a greater fire. Revival fire leads people to the Reviver, Jesus Christ. Every altar where the fire of God is burning becomes a lifeline thrown into the flames of judgment.

You and I are not called to watch this lost world stumble into hell. We are called to intercept them. The revival fire that fills our hearts and our churches isn't a private gift. It's an assignment. When you burn with God's love, you carry God's invitation to salvation into hell's territory. Every word of truth, every act of kindness, and every declaration of the gospel is living water thrown on the flames of eternal death.

This is why revival and awakening are pouring out. It's all for souls. It's God's final call–a final offer before judgment fire.

Outpourings of God's Spirit is God, in His mercy, saying, "There is still time, save them." When revival burns, evangelism becomes urgent and the Church becomes a rescue mission which it was always meant to be.

The reality of hell is the reason revival cannot be optional. If we truly believe that eternity is real, we can't live casually going through the motions. We can't stay silent. The

Holy Spirit, who convicts us of sin, also compels us to save others from it. When we burn for God, we burn with His burden–that none should perish, but all should come to repentance (2 Peter 3:9).

We stand between two fires: the fire of revival and the fire of judgment, and our calling is to pull as many people as possible from judgment into revival. When we burn with holy fire, hell loses its grip. This is why you were set on fire–to carry God's mercy, a message of freedom and salvation, to a world on the edge of eternity.

We must burn for the souls who cannot yet see the danger. We must burn for the ones still asleep in sin. And we must burn now, before it's too late.

THE REALITY OF HELL–THE PLACE WHERE FIRE NEVER DIES

Hell is not a myth, a metaphor, or a story to frighten children. It is the most terrifying reality in existence. It is the final destination of rebellion, the eternal outcome of every "no" ever spoken to the mercy of God. And though the redeemed in Christ are rescued from it, the Church cannot ignore it, forget it, or grow numb to it. Because every lost soul you meet, every neighbor, every coworker, and every face in the crowd is a heartbeat away from this place if they die without Jesus.

Jesus spoke about hell more than any other person in

Scripture, because He alone knew the full horror of it. He called it *"the outer darkness" (Matthew 8:12)*–a realm where there is no light and no love. He said it was a place *"where their worm does not die and the fire is not quenched" (Mark 9:44)*. The worm speaks of conscience that never sleeps. Meaning the worm represents eternal awareness of what could have been, an endless replay of rejecting Christ.

Revelation calls it *"the lake of fire and brimstone" (Revelation 20:10)*–a sea of unending judgment. The smoke of torment rises forever. There are no second chances, there is no relief, and there is no breath of peace. Hell is not ruled by Satan. It is ruled by divine justice. Even the devil will be cast there in final defeat. There, he won't be reigning in power. He will be suffering in punishment. It is the place where all rebellion against God ends in silence and agony.

The story of the rich man and Lazarus in Luke 16 isn't a parable. It is a glimpse into the reality of eternity. The rich man was clothed in luxury all his life but he lifted his eyes in torment the moment he died. He saw things, he felt things, and his memory was fully intact. He begged for a single drop of water to cool his tongue, but not even that could reach him. And what did he ask next? "Please, send someone to warn my brothers." Even from the flames of hell, his only desire was that others would not come to that place. That is the state of every lost soul right now: "Send someone to tell them before it's too late."

Believer of Jesus Christ reading this book right now, that someone is you.

Hell is the most hated truth in the world today. Most don't preach it, and some don't even believe it anymore, even in Pentecostal circles. They say it's incompatible with the preaching of God's love. They say, "How can a God of mercy send anyone to a burning pit of eternal hell?" To that, I say, "If there is no hell, what did Jesus die on The Cross to save us from?" If there is no hell, where the ungodly pay for eternity for their sinful conduct, why is the Bible saturated with that reality from the Old Testament all the way through the New? If there is no hell, why did Moses write about it in Deuteronomy 32:22 saying, *"For a fire is kindled in My anger, and shall burn to the lowest hell?"* If there is no hell, why did King David write in Psalm 9:17, *"The wicked shall be turned into hell, and all the nations that forget God?"* If there is no hell, why did Jesus say in Matthew 5:29–30, *"If your right eye causes you to sin, pluck it out and cast it from you; for it is more profitable for you that one of your members perish, than for your whole body to be cast into hell?"* If there is no hell, why did John the Revelator write in Revelation 20:14, *"Then Death and Hades were cast into the lake of fire?"* If there is no hell, why did Jesus give us the story of the rich man and Lazarus in Luke 16:19–31? Some say it's a parable. This is not a parable. Jesus didn't use first names in parables. These were real people in a real place. There is a living reality beyond this one. It's real. It's living, and it's for eternity. They had self-awareness. They knew who they were and where they were. They knew where other people were.

Everyone of us is going to live forever somewhere. It will either be in the presence of the Lord Jesus Christ, whom we've received, or in a place called hell, because we have denied Him. Those are the only two options.

The truth is that God never did and never will send a person to hell. If someone goes there, it's of their own free will. God doesn't send people to hell. They go there because they reject the redemption of Jesus Christ on The Cross. They send themselves there. Jesus Christ did everything He could to save us. He gave us the way out. God has placed barrier after barrier in the path of every sinner so they would turn to Him, but many choose the path of death rather than the path of life.

Matthew 7:13–14 says, *"Enter by the narrow gate; for wide is the gate and broad is the way that leads to destruction, and there are many who go in by it. Because narrow is the gate and difficult is the way which leads to life, and there are few who find it."*

Jesus preached that. Jesus was saying that the majority of humanity will spend eternity in hell. I didn't make this up. Jesus will be the Judge of all the earth one day, and every one of us will stand in front of Him.

His Word cries out to warn us. Jesus warned us about hell. Jesus preached more about hell than He did about Heaven. Jesus was the greatest preacher on the subject of hell that the world has or will ever see. He preached it in word and lived it in action unto His very death on The Cross of Calvary.

Hell is real. Hell is not just some doctrine to be believed. It is a real place. And you were saved not just so you could escape that place, but to rescue others from ending up there. My question for every believer is this, "Is hell just a doctrine for you or is it a burning reality?" I often say, "The lost need a revelation of The Cross, but believers need a revelation of hell." Allow me a few minutes to provide you with one.

WHAT IS HELL LIKE?

Hell is a kingdom of total darkness–literally and spiritually. It is eternal darkness, deep darkness. In the Kingdom of God there will be no need for a candle or the sun, because the glory of God will be our light. Jesus Christ will shine in His glory. He is the light of those in Heaven. But not so in the kingdom of darkness.

Hell doesn't have an ounce of light. It's so dark that all light is consumed. Lamentations 3:6 says, *"He has set me in dark places, like the dead of long ago."* Jude 13 speaks of *"the blackness of darkness forever."* The darkness there is tormenting and suffocating.

This darkness cannot be fully understood by the mind because we have never experienced eternal darkness. It is utter and complete separation from the presence of God. The reason we can't imagine that is because the Holy Spirit, the

Comforter, is still here on earth and working. Even sinners who don't know God are experiencing a sense of safety and comfort while the Holy Spirit remains here.

The kind of darkness in hell isn't just seen–it's felt. Exodus 10:21 mentions a darkness that could be felt because it was so wicked and evil. It is a complete spiritual emptiness and void–death, no hope, no life, no happiness, and no joy. You might say, "But if there is fire, there must be light." Not in the fires of hell. There is no light in that fire.

Psalm 11:6 says, *"Upon the wicked He will rain coals; fire and brimstone and a burning wind shall be the portion of their cup."* Psalm 140:10 says, *"Let burning coals fall upon them; let them be cast into the fire, into deep pits, that they rise not up again."* Matthew 13:49–50 says, *"The angels will come forth, separate the wicked from among the just, and cast them into the furnace of fire. There will be wailing and gnashing of teeth."*

Hell is a place numbered with the transgressors–full of the worst kinds of sinners the world has ever seen. From the unnamed child molester to Hitler. Can you imagine waking up in that kind of company? Nothing but sinners and the ungodly. Backsliders and compromisers will be there too. For what? For denying Jesus and for choosing to walk in their own way instead of following Him.

Hell is more than just being abandoned by God. Hell is a living place–a burning, conscious reality where the soul will be completely awake and aware of what is happening to them. There are no exits. There are no U-turns.

Hell is a literal prison. Isaiah 24:22 says, *"They will be gathered together, as prisoners are gathered in the pit, and will be shut up in the prison."* Proverbs 7:27 speaks of *"the chambers of death."* Job 17:16 says, *"Will they go down to the gates of Sheol? Shall we have rest together in the dust?"* Jonah 2:6 says, *"The earth with its bars closed behind me forever."* Many commentaries say Jonah was at the very gates of hell, and that these were literal bars and gates.

Hell is hotter than can be imagined–heat beyond anything we can comprehend, heat to such a degree that life cannot be sustained.

Hell will rob all physical strength. The desire to run away will exist but no strength is present to run. It will take every ounce of energy to move even an inch. Isaiah 14:9–10 says, *"Hell from beneath is excited about you, to meet you at your coming; it stirs up the dead for you... They shall speak and say to you, 'Have you also become as weak as we? Have you become like us?'"* Psalm 88:4 says, *"I am counted with those who go down to the pit; I am like a man who has no strength."* Why is there no strength in hell? Because Acts 17:28 says, *"For in Him we live and move and have our being."* Even movement comes from God.

Hell has horrific demons and creatures in it. Revelation 16:13 speaks of demons like frogs. Revelation 9 describes terrible beings coming out of the pit. These entities have an extreme hatred for God and blaspheme Him continually. Revelation 13:6 and James 2:7 teach that blasphemy comes from the demonic realm. These demons and creatures direct their hatred toward God's creation–those who are cast into hell and they torment them day and night.

The pain and torment there will be felt. The pain is literal. After death, a soul does not become some ghost without feeling who forgets who they are. Just as we have an eternal body prepared for those who go to Heaven, there is an eternal body prepared for those who go to hell. Matthew 10:28 says, *"Fear Him who is able to destroy both soul and body in hell."* In Luke 16, the rich man had a tongue and wanted a drop of water to cool it. He had a mouth to speak and eyes he lifted to look upward. Those who are in hell, have a body–a body created to endure torment for all eternity.

Hell has different levels of punishment and degrees of torment. Matthew 23:14 says, *"You will receive greater condemnation."* Matthew 10:15 says, *"It will be more tolerable for Sodom and Gomorrah in the day of judgment than for that city."* Hebrews 10:29 says, *"Of how much worse punishment, do you suppose, will he be thought worthy who has trampled the Son of God underfoot?"* There is worse punishment, but no level is bearable. Even the least is more terrible than the human mind can comprehend. The eternal body created for hell won't even be able to bleed, for Leviticus 17:11 says, *"The life of the flesh is in the blood."* There is no life in hell so there is no blood.

Hell is a place of weeping and gnashing of teeth–a place of absolute torture.

In hell there is no purpose, no identity, and no destiny. Ecclesiastes 9:10 says, *"There is no work or device or knowledge or wisdom in the grave where you are going."* Ecclesiastes 6:4 says, *"Your name is covered in darkness."* Psalm 88:12, Isaiah 26:14, Deuteronomy 32:26, and Psalm 109:15 all speak of being forgotten in hell. It doesn't matter if the person was famous on earth–in hell they are unknown and without identity.

Hell has no water. Thirst can not be quenched and the pain of the heat cannot be eased by even a drop of water. Zechariah 9:11 calls it *"a waterless pit."*

Hell has no air to breathe. Imagine the worst asthma attack you can. Hell is a suffocating reality for all eternity. Why? Because Isaiah 42:5 says, *"The Lord gives breath to the people on it."* Hell is a place beneath the earth; no longer upon the earth.

Hell is a place where sleep is impossible. The desire remains, but rest will never come. Revelation 14:10–11 says, *"They will be tormented with fire and brimstone... and they have no rest day or night."* Rest is a blessing from God. Psalm 127:2 says, *"The Lord gives His beloved sleep."*

Hell has a horrific, rotting smell. Jesus rebuked foul spirits; demons have a foul smell and so does hell.

Hell is a place of absolute fear. Psalm 73:18–19 says, *"You cast them down to destruction. Oh, how they are brought to desolation, as in a moment! They are utterly consumed with terrors."*

Hell is not a place anyone wants to go. Hell is not a myth. Hell is not a place where people will party with their friends.

Hell is not just a symbol or a state of separation from God. Hell is a real place–a burning reality right now. It is a pit filled with millions of souls, burning, terrified, screaming, tormented, weeping, wailing, and gnashing their teeth. They are regretting every moment they denied Jesus.

Their greatest torment is The Cross of Jesus Christ. It may be an offense on earth, but in hell it becomes unbearable–the full story is known. Every soul in hell instantly understands how simple it was: "Believe in Jesus, follow Jesus. Repent and be saved." It was so simple.

My intention in these words is to ensure that you are aware there is a fire burning and millions are rushing toward it. I am sounding an alarm in your path to wake you up to this reality. I pray these words are beating upon your heart and opening your eyes to see that every soul you pass, every single day, could be heading to hell and you could stop that. You could be the mouthpiece God uses to save their soul. You could stand in the way crying, "Run to Jesus and live."

To every blood-bought believer of Jesus Christ, the flame of the Holy Ghost that burns within you is God's answer to hell's fire. You are a torch in a dark world, carrying the same mercy that once pulled you from destruction. When you share Christ, when you tell people, "Jesus loves you, died for you and rose again; He died for your sins and you can be saved today," you interrupt hell's plan.

If the Church truly understood hell, apathy would die instantly. We would never again measure success by attendance but by souls snatched from the flames of judgment. We would stop arguing with one another and start contending for the lost. We would pray with tears, preach with urgency, and live with eternity stamped on our eyeballs. Revival fire burns hottest when it remembers what it saves people from.

Imagine the unending sound of souls crying out in regret–their screams blending with the echo of the gospel they ignored replaying in their memory for all eternity. Imagine the isolation, the darkness so thick it feels alive, the absence of all that is good, and true, and pure. Imagine an eternity knowing you rejected the only Person that could save you. That is the reality of hell, and every believer must face it with a burning compassion that refuses to let others go there unwarned.

God has given us the power to interrupt that path. Through the gospel, the blood of Jesus, and the fire of the Holy Ghost, we carry the cure to eternal death.

When we speak of hell, we don't do it to terrify people. We speak and preach about hell to warn people of the truth and to awaken the Church into action. The love that drove Christ to The Cross, where He descended into death to break its power forever. His cry, "It is finished!" was the declaration that the fires of judgment no longer own us. But it is now our mission to carry the message of The Cross and an empty tomb to those still in chains.

There are souls on your street, in your city, and in your

family who are walking toward eternity without God. They will either be met by the flame of revival through the Church and believers like you or the flame of judgment without us. This thought alone should shake us from every distraction.

I pray a holy urgency ignites in your soul and compels you to witness, to preach, to intercede, and to love and reach the lost. Let the love of God make you fearless and let the fire of God make you relentless. Every soul you reach is one less soul condemned to hell. You have been saved from the fire—now live to save others from it.

The greatest damage you can ever do to the kingdom of darkness is to win a soul and the most compelling witness is one who burns with Holy Ghost fire, power, and conviction.

THE FLAMES OF COMPASSION–BURNING FOR SOULS BEFORE THEY BURN FOREVER

Holy Ghost revival fire is a kind of fire that delivers. It is the burning heart of Christ Himself alive in His people. When the Holy Spirit fills a man or woman, He does more than empower them to speak in tongues or perform miracles. He gives them a burden for the lost.

The fire of compassion is what moved Jesus when He saw the multitudes scattered and lost. "He was moved with compassion for them, because they were weary and scattered, like sheep having no shepherd" (Matthew 9:36). That word *moved* means to be stirred from the deepest core; to feel pain deep in the soul. The Son of God was pierced by the sight of wandering and lost souls but that didn't bring defeat, it motivated Him to action. He healed, preached, fed, delivered, and ultimately gave His life. That same burning ache has invaded the Church of Jesus Christ again.

If revival fire does not lead us to reach out and rescue the lost, it is not revival.

The Holy Spirit doesn't just give believers power to shout in church. He gives them fire to go into the streets, the prisons, the alleys, the schools, and the nations carrying the burning compassion of Jesus Christ like a torch.

When Jesus stood outside Lazarus's tomb, He wept. The tears came before the miracle. That's the pattern of revival. The burden precedes the move of God. Before we can call the dead to life, we must first be moved by their death. When your heart begins to break for those who are spiritually lost, the compassion of Christ has taken hold of you and the fire of God will follow.

The prophet Jeremiah carried that same flame. He cried, "Oh, that my head were waters and my eyes a fountain of tears, that I might weep day and night for the slain of the daughter of my people!" (Jeremiah 9:1). His nation had turned to idols, but he didn't rage in hate. He wept and was burdened. Revival doesn't start in anger; it starts in agony. It begins when the Church hears the cry of the lost louder than the desires of the saved.

Paul carried this burden like a fire in his bones. He said, *"I have great sorrow and continual grief in my heart... for my brethren, my countrymen according to the flesh" (Romans 9:2–3)*. This man who shook cities with miracles also wept over them with compassion. He told the Philippians, *"Many walk... whose end is destruction... and now I tell you even weeping" (Philippians 3:18)*. Paul wasn't building a name for himself. He was emptying hell. His gospel was drenched in tears and burden and forged in the flames of God's love for the lost. That is the fire the Church must operate in.

We need a burden for souls that makes us uncomfortable, interrupts our services, and ruins our agendas. When the compassion of Christ burns in you, you begin to see people not as irritating, but as assignments. Every cashier, every neighbor, and every stranger becomes an eternal soul hanging between Heaven and hell. You start to feel what God feels–that every person you pass was worth shedding the blood of His Son.

Compassion is the most dangerous weapon because it demands action. It can't stay still or silent when the lost are perishing. It moves, it speaks, and it sacrifices. It stands in the gap and it says, "If someone must go, send me." The fire of compassion will make you weep and war at the same time, crying for the broken while confronting the devils that hold them bound.

When compassion ignites conviction, evangelism stops being a program and becomes alive and active. You don't wait for altar calls, you create them everywhere you go. You stop praying for revival and instead, you start living it every day.

This is what drove Jesus to The Cross. It wasn't nails that held Him there. It was love. It was the fire of compassion that would rather die than watch humanity perish. And if the Holy Spirit lives in us, then the compassion of Christ must burn through us until the lost are reached.

This is what must mark the Church, not just a passion for God, but a compassion for lost souls. The kind of burning that won't let us rest while others are perishing. The kind that refuses to let the gospel stop with us but burns for the salvation of lost souls until their names are written in the Book of Life.

LIVING FOR ETERNITY–TRADING EARTHLY PLEASURE FOR HEAVENLY REWARD

Eternity is closer than you think. This life on earth will be over before you know it. Eternity is not a distant dream. It is the backdrop of everything. Every choice, every word, and every hidden motive either builds for eternity or burns away in it. The fire of revival is not just about miracles in the present; it is about living with eternity in sight.

The tragedy of our generation is not ignorance of eternity–it's indifference to it. We plan for careers, for comfort, for retirement, but we rarely plan for forever. Scripture declares, *"What does it profit a man if he gains the whole world, and loses his own soul?"* (Mark 8:36). The worth of eternity cannot be measured by earthly scales. The world's pleasures are momentary compared to eternal glory.

The comforts of this world are deceptive–they promise satisfaction but deliver emptiness. Sin is always short-lived, and compromise always comes with a cost. Revival fire calls us to live with eyes fixed beyond the temporary–to see the unseen and to value the eternal over the immediate. The more you live for eternity, the less this world can control you.

Paul wrote, *"For our light affliction, which is but for a moment, is working for us a far more exceeding and eternal weight of glory"* (2 Corinthians 4:17). That phrase–eternal weight of glory–is the language of Heaven. The pain you endure for Christ now will outshine the pleasures of a thousand lifetimes. Every sacrifice, every act of obedience, every act of service, every moment of surrender, and every prayer carries eternal weight. The fire of revival makes you see that nothing done for Jesus is ever wasted.

The apostles lived as if Heaven was more real than earth. They faced beatings, exile, persecution, and death but their eyes were locked on eternity. Paul declared, *"I have fought the good fight, I have finished the race, I have kept the faith. Finally there is laid up for me the crown of righteousness"* (2 Timothy 4:7–8). He didn't live for applause, he lived for a crown and he gained his reward.

Revival fire shifts your value system. It breaks the addiction to the things of this world that fade away and it ignites a holy hunger for what lasts. When eternity grips your heart, you stop asking, "What can I get away with?" and start asking, "What can I give away for Him?" You realize that pleasure without purpose is absolutely pointless.

Jesus told a story about a rich man who built bigger barns to store his abundance. He said to himself, *"Soul, you have many goods laid up for many years; take your ease; eat, drink, and be merry."* But God said to him, *"Fool! This night your soul will be required of you; then whose will those things be which you have provided?"* (Luke 12:19–20). He lived for the temporary and forfeited the eternal. The barns were full, but his soul was bankrupt.

This world is a vapor. Every life will pass quickly by but eternity is unending. Eternity is forever. Revival fire opens your eyes to see life from Heaven's view. When fire burns in you, eternity becomes your reality. You live differently, you give differently, and you love differently.

In Heaven, there will be no applause for worldly accomplishments, but there will be a reward for loyalty. There will be no trophies for success, but there will be crowns for perseverance. The applause of men will fade, but the approval of Christ, "Well done, good and faithful servant," will remain..

Those who live for eternity become unstoppable. They don't fear death because they've already died to the world. They don't cling to possessions because they've already traded them for a kingdom. They don't bow to the culture because they've already bowed to Jesus, the King of kings and the Lord of lords. When all the kingdoms of this world are gone, when the lights of fame and fortune have gone dark, the fire of the eternal will still burn. And those who lived for eternity will shine like the sun in the Kingdom of their Father forever.

CARRIERS OF ANOTHER WORLD–BRINGING THE ATMOSPHERE OF HEAVEN TO EARTH

When a man or woman burns with the presence of God, they carry more than a message; they carry another world. They become the vessel in which Heaven invades earth.

Heaven is not just a distant place you will visit someday. It is a living reality that already resides within you. Jesus said, *"The Kingdom of God is within you" (Luke 17:21)*. That means the atmosphere of Heaven can break out anywhere through anyone who carries it. When the Holy Spirit fills you, the presence of God fills every room you walk into. Every conversation and environment becomes an opportunity for a divine collision.

The book of Revelation gives us a glimpse of Heaven's atmosphere: flashes of lightning, voices, thunder, and fire before the throne. Angels crying "Holy, Holy, Holy" without rest. A sea of glass reflecting glory. There is no fear there, no sin, no shadow; only endless light and perfect peace. This is the same atmosphere the Holy Spirit plants in the hearts of those who walk with God on earth.

Being filled with the Spirit is not just the power to preach. It's the power to shift the atmosphere. You become a walking sanctuary and a living ambassador of a higher realm. Jesus demonstrated this everywhere He went. When He entered a room, demons screamed and sickness fled. He didn't adjust to the atmosphere around Him. The atmosphere adjusted to Jesus. He carried Heaven in such measure that even His clothes radiated power. The woman with the issue of blood touched the current of the healing power of God running through human flesh.

Too often, believers try to blend in with the world instead of overcoming and transforming it. But those who carry the fire of God can't blend in–they burn. You were not saved to adapt to the darkness around you. You were saved to overcome and dispel it. Jesus called you "the light of the world" and "the salt of the earth." Salt changes whatever it touches. Light cannot mix with darkness. It conquers it. That's what happens when the atmosphere of Heaven invades the earth.

Every believer filled with the Holy Spirit carries the authority of God. That means when you walk into a hospital, Heaven has entered the room. When you walk into a classroom, Heaven has entered the school. When you walk into a broken family, Heaven has stepped into that home. You are a carrier. You bring another world with you. You are a torch of revival fire.

Heaven's atmosphere is tangible and when the fire of revival burns, it releases the atmosphere of Heaven. People can sense it even if they can't explain it. Conviction falls. Hope rises. Chains break. That's what the presence of the Lord does. That's the climate of the kingdom.

We have to stop living like Heaven is far away. The Holy Spirit is Heaven's ambassador living inside of you right now. The fire of God in you is supernatural. It's a miracle. It's the light of eternity. When you walk with the fire of God, you become a living contradiction to the culture around you. You are peace in chaos. You are purity in corruption. You are faith in fear. And you are love in the midst of hatred. You are evidence that another kingdom has come.

You were born to carry the fire and nature of God. You were designed to host God's presence and release His power. You are a carrier of the world to come, walking through the darkness of a dying one, and lighting it up with the light of Christ. It is not enough for you to simply know about Heaven, you must bring it. Wherever you go, Heaven just walked in.

ONE FLAME CAN IGNITE A NATION–THE POWER OF A BURNING LIFE

God doesn't often work through crowds to change history. He works through people. He works through burning lives: one man, one woman; one torch lit by the fire of His presence, refusing to bow, refusing to cool down, and refusing to quit. National revival does not begin in masses–it begins in a single heart that says, "God, set me on fire, and I'll burn until the world around me catches fire." Don't ever underestimate the power of one life on fire. The enemy fears it more than any army, because one burning believer exposes his entire kingdom. The fire in one heart can ignite thousands and become a light that guides a generation.

God doesn't need some famous name or perfect pedigree. He is looking for another vessel. He doesn't need another influencer. He is looking for another intercessor. One person who walks into darkness carrying the fire of God is more powerful than ten thousand Christian spectators. The fire of one life surrendered to God can dismantle hell's systems and call nations back to righteousness.

Never say, "I'm just one person." So was Noah when he built an ark. So was Daniel when he prayed in Babylon. So was Esther when she entered the throne room. Every great move of God started with a life willing to burn. You may feel small, but the fire inside you is not.

The question is not whether you can change the world, the question is whether you will burn long enough for God to use you. Fire always spreads. It just needs something to consume. It will continue to burn as long as you feed it, as long as you continue to surrender everything, and as long as you keep your eyes fixed on eternity and your heart fixed on

Jesus. When you let His fire consume you, the fire will spread from your life to others until whole cities burn with glory.

Believers of Jesus Christ do not blend into the darkness. We ignite it and overcome it.

You may not be able to reach everyone, but the fire in you can reach someone and that someone can reach someone else. This is how revival spreads. This is how darkness is devoured. That is how Heaven's Kingdom advances.

One flame. One life. One yes to God.

And, because you burned with revival fire until the darkness broke, the world will never be the same.

CONCLUSION

A war is raging for the souls of mankind. We have already established that fact in this book. And every believer is drafted into this conflict–not to spectate, but to fight. We're not wrestling flesh and blood but the rulers of darkness, the architects of deception, and the unseen forces poisoning an entire generation.

This generation is bleeding in spirit. Many have never heard the truth of the gospel, and others have heard a powerless version that never cut deep enough. The spirit of this age whispers, "There's still time," while eternity screams, "Time is running out."

When revival fire burns in a believer, you begin to see through God's eyes. The atheist isn't your enemy; he's a captive. The addict isn't a statistic; she's a prisoner who needs a rescuer. The rebellious aren't beyond reach; they're targets of God's mercy. We have to war for a generation before hell owns it. That means confronting lies with truth and confronting darkness with light. It means standing between God's justice and man's rebellion with the fire of compassion and the sword of truth.

Jesus Himself was a warrior for the lost. Every miracle was an act of war. Every deliverance was a declaration that the kingdom of darkness was losing ground. He entered enemy-occupied territory–synagogues filled with demons, streets filled with disease, tombs filled with death and He turned them into altars of deliverance.

His Spirit burns in you. The authority that drove out demons in Galilee can drive them out through you today. When you open your mouth to declare truth, darkness has to flee. When you pray with fire, strongholds shatter. When you step into the world as a burning vessel of God, you carry the invasion of Heaven wherever you go.

Do not underestimate the urgency of this hour. The enemy is not waiting, and neither can we. The warriors of revival do not wear armor for show. They wear it for battle. Their prayers are weapons. Their words are fire. Their lives are living proof that Jesus still saves. They don't wait for the lost to wander into church. They carry the Church into the world. They go and they get them.

We must stand in the gap before it's too late, weep over

our cities, and intercede for our generation. It's time to preach the gospel like it's the last thing we'll ever say. Time is collapsing and eternity is approaching.

The enemy has unleashed everything he can but he cannot overcome a burning Church; one that refuses to back down, refuses to blend in, refuses to quit, and refuses to stop fighting for souls. This is what the gates of hell cannot prevail against–a Church on fire, warring for the lost until the last breath.

THE COMING GLORY–LIVING FOR THE DAY WHEN HEAVEN BREAKS THROUGH

All of this is pointing toward one ultimate moment–the day when Heaven fully breaks through. This is the promise of Scripture. The return of King Jesus is certain. Jesus Christ, who ascended, will return in glory, and when He does, the world will see the purpose behind everyone who ever burned for Him.

We are not laboring for nothing. We are not burning for something temporary. We are burning for the day when the eastern sky splits open, when time folds into eternity, and when the glory of God covers the earth like the waters cover the sea.

One day, Jesus Himself, the Lord strong in battle, will break through the heavenly realm and descend.

Jesus said in John 14:1-3:

"Let not your heart be troubled; you believe in God, believe also in Me. In My Father's house are many mansions; if it were not so, I would have told you. I go to prepare a place for you. And if I go and prepare a place for you, I will come again and receive you to Myself; that where I am, there you may be also."

His name is Jesus Christ of Nazareth, and He said He's coming back. As I watch the events of the world unfold, how much closer are we to His return? The King is coming!

Paul said creation itself groans for that day (Romans 8:22). The earth trembles, longing for the revealing of the sons and daughters of God. Heaven is not distant. It is pressing closer. The hand of God is heavy upon us. His weight is pressing down because in His grace, He desires that none should perish but all would know Him. The early Church lived in constant anticipation of Christ's return. They preached with urgency and died with joy because they knew something the modern Church has forgotten: this world is not our home. They looked for a city whose builder and maker is God. Their eyes were fixed not on Rome's power, but on Heaven's promise. That is what revival fire restores, an eternal focus that can't be shaken.

The coming glory is not about escape. It's about completion. When Jesus returns, the fire we carried in part will become fullness. The light we glimpsed in revival will flood the universe. The Lamb who was slain will be seen as King, crowned in majesty, and every knee will bow, and every tongue will confess that He is Lord. Every act of faith and soul won will shine like jewels in the crown of His glory.

But until that day, the glory has been entrusted to us. Jesus said, *"The glory which You gave Me I have given them, that they may be one just as We are one" (John 17:22)*. The presence that fills Heaven dwells in the believer. Revival fire is for now. We are not waiting for the glory to come. We are carriers of it. Revival is not only the hope of nations. It is the preview of eternity. When the Church burns with the presence of God, the world gets a glimpse of the kingdom to come.

When you spend time in the fire of God's presence, something of eternity marks you. You begin to live differently and see things differently. You carry the coming world within you.

One day soon, the veil will lift. The skies will burn with brilliance. The trumpet will sound. The King of Glory will descend with fire in His eyes, and the fire we have carried will answer His. Until then, every flame on earth is a signal, "He's coming." Every revival is preparation for His return. Every believer burning with His presence is a forerunner preparing the way of the Lord.

Live for that glorious day. Work while it is still day–the night is coming when no one can work. Let everything you do for Him be aimed toward the moment when Heaven and earth collide in restoration.

The coming glory is our destiny. The light within you is proof that Heaven is close. The fire you carry is the heat of eternity breaking through the veil.

Soon the battle will end. The war for souls will cease. The Church triumphant will stand before the Lamb, torches in hand, faces shining with everlasting light. The fire that once burned through us in our weakness will now burn in fullness around His throne.

And in that moment, when Heaven breaks through, everything will make sense–the fire, the tears, the fight, the waiting. We will know it was worth it all.

He's coming.

And every flame that still burns when He does will burn forever with Him.

THE LAST CALL

This is it. The last call before the final conflict. The line between Heaven and hell is drawn. The world is at war for souls, and the call has gone out across the earth, "Burn until the darkness breaks."

There is no backup plan. There is no one else coming. You are Heaven's answer to the crisis of your generation. The same Spirit that raised Jesus from the dead lives in you. You carry the same power that crushed the grave. The same Spirit that fell on Pentecost burns in your bones.

You are standing in a moment that prophets only saw from a distance–the final stretch of the story, when the Church becomes what she was always meant to be: an unbreakable army of burning men and women who refuse to retreat.

So here's the order: take your post and hold the ground. Preach the gospel when the world forbids it. Stand for truth when it costs you your name and reputation. Protect the next generation when hell targets them. Refuse the lies. Reject the fear. Tear down the idols.

Push back the darkness until it breaks.

You don't fight for victory. You fight from it. The cross already broke the back of the enemy. The resurrection already sealed the victory. You are not trying to win. You are enforcing what Jesus already accomplished.

Don't wait for the right time–this is the time. Don't wait for another generation–you are the generation.

Now is the hour to fight for your families.

To fight for your cities.

To fight for the gospel.

To fight for the glory of God.

To fight for revival and awakening in the land of the living.

When it's over and the smoke clears, let it be written of

us, "They didn't flinch. They didn't fold. They didn't fade. They burned until the darkness broke."

And when the King returns in glory, may He find His Church ready–fire in our eyes, conviction in our voices, and a holy flame still burning in our hearts.

This is the last call. Burn until the darkness breaks.

"People are dying. Jesus is coming. What we do, we must do quickly" –Brian Bolt

SALVATION'S CALL

THE GREATEST DECISION OF YOUR LIFE

All the revival fire in the world means nothing if you have never encountered Jesus Christ as your personal Lord and Savior.

You may have read these pages and felt the stirring of God's presence, but this journey must always begin in one place–at the cross.

Every one of us was born separated from God by sin. No matter how good we try to be, we cannot save ourselves. But God, in His mercy, sent His Son, Jesus Christ, to take our place–to bear our sin, to pay a debt he didn't owe; a debt we couldn't pay. On The Cross of Calvary, Jesus died for our sins. He took on the punishment and judgment for our sins so we wouldn't have to be separated from God anymore. His death gave us the ability to be forgiven and to receive life in Him, now and for eternity. He died so we could live.

Then three days later, He rose from the dead, proving that sin and death had been defeated forever. Jesus saves and Jesus lives!

"For all have sinned and fall short of the glory of God."– Romans 3:23

"But God demonstrates His own love toward us, in that while we were still sinners, Christ died for us."–Romans 5:8

"That if you confess with your mouth the Lord Jesus and believe in your heart that God has raised Him from the dead, you will be saved."–Romans 10:9

Jesus is not a dead, religious, crucified man–He is a living, resurrected, all powerful Savior.

He is not far away–He is right here, waiting for you. He offers forgiveness, freedom, and eternal life to anyone who will call on His name. No sin is too great. No past is too dark. No life is too far gone.

Right now, this very moment, you can begin again.

If you've never surrendered your life to Jesus Christ, or if you've drifted from Him and know it's time to come home, this is your moment.

He's reaching out to you right now.

You don't have to fix yourself first–just come as you are. He will take your sin and give you His righteousness. He will take your shame and fill you with His peace. He will take your past and give you a brand-new future. You will become a brand new creation in Him.

> *"Therefore if anyone is in Christ, he is a new creation; old things have passed away; behold, all things have become new."–2 Corinthians 5:17*

The most important decision of your entire life begins with one prayer–to make Jesus the Lord of your life.

THE PRAYER OF SALVATION

If you're ready to receive Him, pray this prayer from your heart:

"Lord Jesus, I come to You today.

I know that I am a sinner and I need Your forgiveness.

I believe You died on The Cross for me and rose again from the dead.

Today, I turn away from my sin and I surrender my life to You.

Come into my heart, Lord Jesus.

Be my Savior and my Lord.

Fill me with Your Holy Spirit and set my heart on fire for You.

From this day forward, I will follow You and live for You.

In Jesus' name, Amen."

WELCOME TO THE FAMILY OF GOD

If you prayed that prayer and meant it, you are now a child of God.

Your past is forgiven. Your name is written in Heaven.

The same Spirit that raised Jesus from the dead now lives in you.

"But as many as received Him, to them He gave the right to become children of God."–John 1:12

This is the beginning of your new life in Christ.

Get connected to a Spirit-filled church, spend time in prayer and in the Word, and tell others what God has done for you. You are no longer who you were–you are born again. And as the fire of God grows in you, remember this:

You are now a carrier of revival fire–a living testimony that Jesus saves, heals, and restores. The same fire that touched your heart today will touch the world through you.

Welcome to a new life in Christ. Welcome to the family of God. Welcome home.

ABOUT THE AUTHOR

Brian Bolt is a man on divine assignment–commissioned by Heaven to reach the lost and advance the Kingdom of God in this generation. A former addict and atheist, Brian encountered the saving power of Jesus Christ in the back of an ambulance after surviving a gunshot wound to the head. That moment of mercy marked the beginning of a radical transformation and an unshakable call to preach the gospel to the nations.

After his conversion, Brian attended Bible college, entered full-time ministry, and became a lead pastor–a role he has faithfully served in for more than two decades. His preaching carries the fire of revival and the conviction of a man who has seen the hand of God rescue him from the brink of death. He burns to awaken the Church and raise up a generation of Spirit-filled leaders who walk in bold faith, Holy Ghost power, and Pentecostal fire. His spiritual lineage traces through revival history–marked by the faith of Smith Wigglesworth, the prophetic insight of Howard Carter, the apostolic missions of Lester Sumrall, and the global vision of Dr. Rod Parsley.

Brian is the president and founder of Brian Bolt World Evangelism, a global movement proclaiming the message of Jesus Christ through evangelistic crusades, international missions, and media ministry.

Together with his wife, Natalie, Brian pastors CityReach Church in Whittier, California–a faith-filled, miracle-centered church with a vision to Reach LA and Reach the World. From the streets of Los Angeles to crusade fields across the nations, they have witnessed the miraculous: the hungry fed, the lost saved, the blind see, the deaf hear, the lame walk, the oppressed delivered, and the sick healed.

Brian Bolt is calling forth a Bible-believing, blood-bought, fire-baptized Remnant Army–a generation that will not bow, will not burn out, and will not back down until revival fire sweeps across the earth.

NOTES

Carter, Howard. *Questions & Answers on Spiritual Gifts.* Harrison House : Assemblies of God Pub. House, 1976.

Finney, Charles. *Lectures on Revival of Religion by Charles G. Finney.* Milner, 1839.

The Holy Bible. Thomas Nelson, 2017.

Jessie Penn-Lewis, and Evan Roberts. *War on the Saints.* Thomas E Lowe Ltd, 1973.

Seymour, William Joseph, and Roberts Liardon. *The Great Azusa Street Revival: The Life and Sermons of William Seymour.* Whitaker House, 2020.

Sumrall, Lester. *Christian Foundations*. Sumrall Publishing, 2006.

Wesley, John, and Kenneth J. Collins. *The Sermons of John Wesley: A Collection for the Christian Journey*. Abingdon Press, 2013.

Wigglesworth, Smith. *Ever Increasing Faith*. Start Publishing LLC, 2012.

Woodworth-Etter, Maria Beulah. *Spirit Filled Sermons*. M.B. Woodworth-Etter, 1921.

www.ingramcontent.com/pod-product-compliance
Lightning Source LLC
Chambersburg PA
CBHW070534170426
43200CB00011B/2421